THE FIRST
100 DAYS

Leading Small Non-Profits Out of the Wilderness

THE FIRST
100 DAYS

Leading Small Non-Profits Out of the Wilderness

Zoot Velasco
Illustrated by Robert Stack

Acknowledgments

This book is dedicated to the three non-profit arts managers who inspired me to go into this field: Michael Alexander, Denise Nelson Nash and Lucero Arellano; to my wife, Monette, who has made me a better person and thereby, a better leader; and to Forrest L. Story, Jeffrey Wilcox, CFRE, and all those who provided me training to be a more effective manager.

Table of Contents

The Secular Missionary

Introduction

There's nowhere you can be that isn't where you're meant to be.

—John Lennon & Paul McCartney

In spite of being born in a blizzard, contracting pneumonia, and then being burned in a house fire—all before I was ten days old—I live a very charmed life.

I was born sickly. My mother brought me home from the hospital and draped my crib with a sheet, rubbed me with Vicks VapoRub, and set a vaporizer next to my crib. While my family was at church, the vaporizer dried up and burned, catching my crib on fire. I was ten days old and so small that my dad (who was sleeping in the next room) held me in his hands and ran water over my body with the kitchen faucet. I was burned over 80 percent of my tiny newborn body. I spent the next five years living in the hospital. I lost the skin and muscles in my right foot. I had skin grafts, hair transplants, and muscle operations, but the latter failed and I never regained my muscles. I was in and out of the hospital until I was seventeen.

I had a lot of time to watch TV, and I spent my childhood watching the Fred and Ginger films, Shirley Temple and Bojangles, and Gene Kelly with anybody. I wanted dance lessons, but my mother said no because I still had thigh-high metal braces on my right leg. That didn't stop me from dancing on crutches and even in a wheelchair while healing from a surgery. When I turned twelve, I traded in my metal braces for a new thermoplastic brace that went under the shoe. I could do things I couldn't do before. At this time a new dance craze hit our New York neighborhood. Today we call it break dancing, but then it was called "burnin'" because the object was to burn the other guy in a battle. I would go home at night and practice break dancing in front of my mirror. My favorite dance was the robot. I could identify. My favorite TV show at the time was "The Six Million Dollar Man" with Steve Austin. "We can rebuild him. We have the technology. We can make him better than he was. Faster. Stronger. Better." And I figured with the hospital bills, Blue Cross had at least six million in me! I had to be part robot.

One day I got up the nerve to dance in front of people for the first time at a school dance because I liked this girl who would only dance with guys who could dance. I did a robot dance. All that time practicing paid off. After my first public dance, I got applause! I was accepted for the first time in my life. I got a girlfriend. And I was moving up in the world. But our family moved around a lot, and I never settled down for any period of time.

A Mime with a Mission

I got into managing arts non-profits the same way I get into everything in my life—for all the wrong reasons. But like everything else in my life, I ended up doing what I was meant to do, and for the right reasons.

I started out as a kid wanting to be a missionary priest who traveled the world helping people in villages. While other kids played G.I. Joe, I was Father Damien helping lepers on Molokai. In seventh grade I bought a priest shirt with the Roman collar and wore it to school (it did not really endear me to the other kids). Even as I took the beating for my fashion statements, I offered it up for sins and got some fun out of playing the martyr. I was a strange kid.

But after seeing my classmate's sister Colleen bending over a stove in pink hot pants in 1976 when I was twelve, I had an epiphany. I realized I would never see the priesthood. I decided that I was going to be a wildlife biologist and live in Alaska's Brooks Range at the Arctic Circle. (I was always a dramatic sort with a penchant for doing good works while having an adventure.) So I studied hard and got a scholarship to college in 1980 for wildlife biology from the Isaac Walton League. While my scholarship paid for the books, it did not pay for anything else, so I became a fry cook for Kentucky Fried Chicken for $3.50 an hour. While working there, I saw an ad on the school bulletin board calling for dancers for a new disco dance troupe:

DANCERS, DANCERS, DANCERS NEEDED!
No experience necessary. Will train.
$25 an HOUR!

I auditioned.

There were, however, a few things the ad did not mention about this dance company. The "$25 an hour" was actually $25 for a one-hour show; they did one show a month. Also, you had to understudy for six months before you could get paid. But I went anyway, and I'm glad because it changed my life. I understudied the mime in the dance company, and before a year was out, I was making more money dancing and performing as a mime than if I had graduated in my major, so I dropped out of college and spent the next twelve years as a professional dancer.

I may have gotten into dance to get a girl. I may have gotten into dancing as a profession to make money. But once I started hanging around with artists who were caught up in the creation of work, I was hooked. I studied acting and theatre improvisation at Second City West. I understudied great artists and collaborated with many others. I learned my craft. (Eventually I went back to school and received my degree in dance.)

Visions of Grandeur

I moved to Los Angeles to work in films, like everyone else

in my profession. I worked in a dozen films as an extra before getting my SAG card in a film not worth mentioning. I made commercials, music videos, and two pilots, and I was a regular dancer on a TV show produced by Arsenio Hall. I worked with Michael Jackson and Prince, and I'll never forget those experiences. But it didn't take more than a couple of years for me to realize I hated working in films. The work was not creative; the people were often mean, cruel, and small minded. This was not what I was expecting. It was high school all over again.

One day I had a vision. I was working as a mannequin model for a fashion show at a store opening, and I had gone to the wrong entrance to the store at 9 a.m. No one was there. A limo pulled up. The driver told me I was on the wrong side. The artist entrance was on the other side. He had just dropped off some soap opera celebrities for the opening. He said, "Get in. I'll take you around." I was excited because I had never been in a limo. We drove to the other side, and there were three hundred people or more screaming as this limo pulled into view. I got out, and I was mobbed by the fans. I hear them saying, "Who is he?" "Is he the new character?" "I don't care; get his autograph." I could see what my life would have been like if I were very successful as a performer, and I didn't like it. If that happened to me every time I left my house, if every fight with a girlfriend was in the paper, every act scrutinized, I would go nuts. I realized I didn't like the goal any more than the getting to it. I also realized that the most fun I had at work was when I worked for non-profits teaching theatre to kids, performing at school assemblies, and performing at benefits. The people were amazing, genuine, and happy. The work was fantastic, creative, and meaningful. So from that day in 1992, I stopped trying to work in the "industry" and started trying to have a career in non-profits. That was the best decision I ever made.

For the next two decades, I've had an amazing career doing fabulous things with great people. I spent three years as an artist-in-residence in schools, juvenile halls, and prisons. I received the first National Endowment for the Arts (NEA) grant in a shopping mall at a time when gang shootings made the mall a dangerous place to be. (I found out how many homeless youth live in shopping malls.) I worked on the riot recovery program in Watts after the LA riots in 1992. I founded and worked in the earthquake recovery program in ten shelters after the 1994 Northridge earthquake. I was a production assistant at the 1994 World Cup in Pasadena where I took care of our guest presenter, Ray Bradbury (one of my favorite authors). I was able to produce and perform in the 1994 LA Festival.

Administration Rocks!

While working in non-profits, I found three administrators who inspired me to become an arts administrator: Lucero Arellano at the California Arts Council, Michael Alexander at Grand Performances, and Denise Nelson Nash at Plaza De La Raza (now at Caltech's theatre). All three were amazing at what they did, and I could see how many people they affected by their work. I asked each to mentor me.

By 1994 I had transitioned to an arts administrator position, and I spent the next six years running a prison arts program. I created a ninety-nine-seat theatre, a video studio and a music studio inside the California Rehabilitation Center, a drug treatment prison. I'm proud to say my program produced the first music CDs in a CA state prison, a youth deterrent program in the form of a play, and handmade books that are now at the J. Paul Getty Museum and the Library of Congress. While at the prison, I won a fellowship with leadership training from the California Arts Council and Coro Southern California. Our project was to revamp and consult on the grants process at the City of Los Angeles.

I left prison work in 2000, just as the program was getting diluted from political changes going on in the state. I left to run art centers for the City of Los Angeles Cultural Affairs Department. I was in charge of two art spaces (an old firehouse and a storefront in the harbor city of San Pedro), and two new art centers being built (Banning's Landing and the Croatian Cultural Center). I had old spaces, no budget, and no existing non-profit support groups. I also supervised four art festivals in the harbor that we funded and six partnered art centers that were all over the city, some more than sixty miles away.

At each of my government jobs, I got in trouble for doing too much. With a few exceptions, government supervisors didn't like it when I did a lot of work because it made them do a lot of work. I am much more suited for non-profits that expect everyone to do a lot of work.

It was a great experience, but I wasn't cut out for government work. I became a consultant instead. I liked coming into a place, fixing things, and leaving as they said, "Who was that masked man?" I fixed broken or growing dance companies, theatre companies, youth centers, and art centers. To date, I have been part of more than $10 million in art projects, securing funding through grants, sponsorships, fundraisers, and restructuring. At the helm of The Unusual Suspects Theatre Company, which provides theatre programs in juvenile halls and foster care, I led a campaign that took the organization from an $80,000 budget with one site to a $650,000 budget on five sites, in sixteen months. I have created three non-profits myself. At Homeland Cultural Center in Long Beach, I doubled the programs, patrons, and fundraising in fifteen months.

At the helm of my current center, The Muckenthaler Cultural Center in Fullerton (which we affectionately refer to as "the Muck"), we have tripled patrons, programs, and members in three years, doubled the budget, and brought grants and contracts for education programs from $0 to almost $300,000 per year. Audiences increased from five hundred to more than eleven thousand. Students increased from one thousand to more than eight thousand. The results have been dramatic, especially given that they happened during the worse depression since the New Deal, with non-profits losing 20 percent of their income nationwide. I don't tell you these things to brag. I want you to know I have been where you are and have come out on the other side.

The New Mission

I didn't write this book because wisdom just flows from me innately. I have continually studied arts education, curriculum writing, supervision and management, leadership, and fundraising, from programs through the Association of Fundraising Professionals (AFP), the California Arts Council, the City of Long Beach, Coro, and Executive Service Corps. I have read scores of books on the subject. I am a certified fundraising executive (CFRE), a CPA-like certification from AFP for fundraising.

After thirty years in the arts, I have come back to what I wanted to be when I started: a missionary. Only my mission has changed. I have become a secular missionary. I have seen the arts change lives in substantial ways, and I want to be a catalyst for that. We are missionaries changing the world one community organization at a time. Everything comes down to the mission. If that stays number one in your mind, you can't fail.

The same problems come up over and over again. This book is meant to help you lead a non-profit to success by setting it (and you) up for success in the first one hundred days.

S = LMV
(Success = Leadership, Mission, and Vision)

This book will give you a guide through this formula. It works.

I have written this book in a simple way, as a letter from one man in the trenches to a fellow warrior. This isn't a textbook written in an ivy-covered classroom. These are real-life stories for dealing with real-life issues, designed for those of us working on the front line who don't have the time or money to go to trainings given by people who haven't run a non-profit in years. Are you ready?

Let's start with leadership. Many are chosen, but few will lead.

Leadership: Setting the Mood and Attitude for Growth

Leadership is the art of getting someone else to do something you want done because he wants to do it.
— Dwight D. Eisenhower

I was not a born leader. Quite the contrary, I was not very popular at all as a child. Having been a burn victim with braces on my leg, bald patches in my hair, and scars, I was not the cool kid at school. To make matters worse, I overcompensated by trying to be funny. I spent most of my childhood alone, and although I learned to entertain myself, I had a hard time making friends. I wasn't a leader then; I couldn't even be a follower if I wanted to be. I was the definition of "fringe."

This was not a disadvantage during my twelve-year career as a performer, but it was when I started supervising and managing others. I was horrible at it. Luckily, leadership is a craft, not an art, in that it can be taught. Being a performer gave me the advantage of being a good public speaker who could entertain a group of people. But it was much harder to be IN the group than in front of it, and even worse to LEAD the group.

My first experience in supervision came while running an art program in a state prison. I supervised inmate clerks, so the mistakes I made were with prisoners who weren't in a position to complain. I often denied their requests because I didn't know how to do it, and I didn't want to admit any ignorance among these hard-core criminals. It wasn't until I admitted I was as clueless as they were that we really started to get somewhere and they chose me to lead them. They chose me not because I was wise but only because I had keys, could use a computer, and had the authority to get things done. That is an important distinction. They were a captive audience through which I could learn supervision.

Since the first hundred days is your time frame for success, than your first ten days is your time frame to set the tone for leadership. Here are ten things you should know to establish yourself as a leader:

1. Leadership Is Not Giving Orders

You are the leader not because you are endowed with some great gift but merely because someone believed in your ability, gave you the authority, and put you in charge. But you are not magically "in charge." You do not have all the answers. Saying to staff, "You do as I say and no one will get hurt" isn't leadership—or even management. It's dictatorship. And while some dictators have been able to hold power for some time, most are overthrown or assassinated. Dictatorship isn't the image most non-profits want.

2. You Have One Hundred Days to Prove Yourself

You have been chosen to lead presumably because someone in authority believed in your ability. That doesn't necessarily mean those under you believe in your ability. You have a short window of time—approximately ninety to one hundred business days, which is roughly five months—when respect is given you solely because you are in charge. Once that window closes, you must earn it. If that time elapses and you are not respected as a leader, you never will be at that organization. It's important to make this time count. Sometimes if an organization is going through a restart in which you have been at the helm performing poorly, and you admit you are as clueless as they are but willing to change, they may give you a reboot of a hundred days to show you can turn them around. This situation makes it even more crucial that you show positive leadership.

You can make more sweeping changes without many problems during the first one hundred days than at any other time. One of my mentors, Forrest Story, once told me that there are only two ways to change things: like a hurricane or through evolution. In a hurricane, you wipe everything out and start over; this takes a long time to rebuild. In evolution, change comes very slowly over a long period of time. There is no middle ground. I find that to be largely true, with the exception of the first hundred days. When a new executive comes in to lead a failing organization or that group wants a reboot, people want and expect change. But be careful what you change. If your changes do not make a positive difference in that first hundred days, your leadership will be questioned.

There is one situation in which a hurricane is warranted. If you are taking over an organization after a major scandal or criminal investigation that has been made public, you may need to clean house and start over. The community will not see the organization as renewed without drastic changes. I took a position in such a situation once. I fired everyone (they were all contractors) and made them re-interview for their job. They started calling me the headhunter, but it worked. The program was quickly revitalized without the scent of scandal because it was completely revamped in a very public way.

3. You Must Have Consensus

When traveling inside a dark tunnel where no one knows the way, the leader isn't the one barking orders. The leader is the one they let hold the flashlight and go first. So if an attacking, hungry bear comes out to eat someone, the bear will eat the leader first. Someone else then becomes the leader. The leader's job is to gather opinions and reach consensus on which direction everyone wants to go. The next step is to lead the team into that tunnel. Leadership is about putting yourself out there as bear bait and taking risks for the team. Once you have resigned yourself to that, you can walk without fear. You can also feel good knowing your team will cry at your funeral and proudly say, "He was a great leader before the bear ate him! I would have followed him anywhere." Your team will complain about you. They may say, "That jackass has no clue where he is going." But they are secretly happy that you are the one going first into the dark with no weapons but a flashlight. And they will follow you anywhere when you ask them where they want to go and get consensus on going there. Most people want to feel they have input but don't want to go first. By leading with consensus, you protect their egos and still allow them to feel involved.

When you find your way out of the tunnel, they will say, "It was my idea to go this direction. I saved us!" And when you get lost in a deep abyss, they will say, "Our leader got us lost." They will complain about you when you fail and take credit for your success. But if you are successful in escaping the tunnel, you will be a hero— until the next tunnel comes.

So how do you reach consensus? I figured this out on one of my first successes as a leader. It was a very hard thing to learn and took me years to figure out what was actually a very simple solution. Are you ready for this great pearl of wisdom?

Ask People Their Opinion

That's it. Did you blink and miss it? It's a very simple concept. You'd be surprised at how many managers and leaders don't do this simplest of things because they think their job is to be the patriarch and know everything.

4. Decipher the Code

Interviewing your new staff will help you assess the current environment. And if they are not bitter, they can be a huge asset. At one cultural center, the much-loved founder of the program handpicked me to succeed her. They were big shoes to fill. She was a community legend and a great leader. I took each staff member and volunteer in my office one at a time and got to know them a bit. I learned working in prison that people are much more open and honest with you one-on-one than in a group. Then I asked each this question: "What would you do if you were in my shoes, coming in as the new director?" I have done this at every job since. The answers will surprise you. Some people use this time to talk ill of a colleague. Others use it to let out pent-up feelings of the outgoing director. But at every job where I have done this, most people end up saying the same universal truths that are the heart of the problems, such as:

"Get rid of so-and-so!" There is a personality problem in this organization holding them back (and everyone knows it). You will have to deal with the person who is affecting everything and everyone.

"If I were director, I would make more stuff to do. We don't really do anything except pick up a paycheck and pretend we're helping people." This organization has been cruising on autopilot and is disconnected with both the mission and the problems that exist in the community they should be addressing.

"Our biggest problem was the outgoing director. He/she pissed everyone off. I guess I would try to get all the people he/she alienated back." This organization has to reach out to stakeholders who left and heal old wounds.

"I'd go find someone who can bring some money in because we are broke and in debt." Money is usually never the actual problem. The real problem is budgeting, bad management, and a disconnection with mission. But starting in the red is never good, and that will be the first problem to address.

"So-and-so on our board always shoots down our ideas." Depending on the type of organization and the culture there, people may be blunt and very honest. And you must make it safe for them to do that. Make sure they understand the conversation is confidential. Many times people are waiting for an outsider to come in and change things.

This process will also help you figure out the culture of the organization and the personalities of the staff.

Are they in survival mode? Are they being brought down by one individual? Are they held back by loyalty to a founder who is burned out and in a holding pattern? Have they gotten heavily involved with a program or fundraiser that doesn't serve the mission but now runs the whole organization? These are not uncommon themes.

In some cases a staff member may have been up for your job. This interview will help you find out if they are threatened by you or just want things to be better. They may become your best asset or your biggest liability. Are they jealous enough to try to sabotage you? Or are they hoping you might mentor them?

5. Take Stock

Spend the first two weeks at a new post learning the lay of the land by becoming an expert on your new organization while interviewing "stakeholders." Stakeholders are the people who are key to the success of the organization (either by ability or by title). This includes:

- All paid staff
- All board members
- Committed volunteers
- Committed alumni of the organization programs
- Financial and in-kind investors (donors)
- Key clients/patrons/participants

In this book I refer to donors (those who contribute

funds to an organization) as "investors" because they are not giving away money with no expectations but investing in their community. It's an important distinction in the way you and your organization work with investors and how they perceive you. We will discuss this more throughout the book.

Besides interviewing all the major stakeholders, you must learn the story and history of your organization. You can't just read it. You must study it and know it as if it were your own family history. This is usually a fascinating process and can help you get excited about the organization. There are things you will find out that will help you in many ways later. People are much more willing to follow a leader who is well informed. You will start to live and breathe the organization.

Don't forget to interview community members not associated with your organization and discover the perception in the community about your organization. Does it have a great reputation? Is it the subject of gossip or scandal? Is it unknown to many who should know it? All of these scenarios would be important to know in your first couple weeks. You could even take a street poll. At my current position at my beloved Muckenthaler Cultural Center, which we will refer to henceforth as "the Muck," I took a street poll at a farmer's market my first week. I stopped random strangers. I told them I was taking a poll and asked if they knew the Muckenthaler. Interestingly I got one of three responses almost every time. A third thought it was a private club, a third had an old childhood memory of it, and a third had not heard of it. For an organization that had been in the community for more than forty years, this told me a great deal: We needed to work on our image and mission in ways that would erase the "private club" image and make us known and needed.

Know the basics from which you are starting financially, such as budget, deficits if any, grants written and received, and endowment. Know major investors on your side and those who have fallen away. Set up lunches with them to get their input. It's a great chance to get them onboard. This is all information you should be able to get from staff and your board treasurer. (And because of your interviews, you also know all stakeholders, including staff and their abilities.)

Make this your only priority your first two weeks. It's a lot to expect that ten days into your job you should learn all this, but it will pay big dividends later. Remember, you only have one hundred days.

6. Develop Your Inner Circle

Toward the end of your second week or the start of your third, call a group meeting of your "inner circle." Insiders are key supporters who will help you get things done. It should include all managerial and full-time staff (If staff are not supporting you yet, at least reluctantly, you may have a problem), key board members who support you, and anyone else who believes in you and the organization and either has power (such as a key investor) or special skills (like a volunteer webmaster). In this closed-door meeting, discuss how you interpret the feedback without mentioning specific names or experiences. This will tell the group they are your "go-to guys," your confidants. By addressing them in this way, you let them know they are special to you and your "brain trust." The meeting isn't to tell them anything but to discuss WITH them your interpretation of your findings of the first two weeks.

You might find that people didn't know others felt the same as they. They will be impressed at how much you have learned and how much you value their input, which will build their respect for you. You are developing a team here; you are developing loyalty to you by your confiding in them. Once you have everyone working together toward a goal of fixing the problems at the organization, real progress can begin.

This first inner-circle meeting is very important. Don't feel bad if some of your interpretations of their feelings miss the mark. They will let you know when you misinterpret things. This is a good time to correct course. You are setting the precedent that you believe in communication and consensus with your inner circle. You are mentoring them subconsciously to be the same way with their inner circles.

7. Fight Pettiness with Professionalism

There is usually a person who is negative or who will clash with new leadership. If you deal with such people professionally and respectfully, the team will usually marginalize them and they will tend to leave on their own accord, which is the best-case scenario for you and the organization. Sometimes it's not so clean a break, and you may have to dismiss someone. But if you have been above board and respectful, then even if they bad-mouth you after leaving, you will be Teflon because you have a whole team of witnesses who will take your side.

You might find one stakeholder resistant, angry, or uncooperative. This person probably is poisoning the well for others. Never address this person in the group. Ask to see him or her one-on-one. I learned working in prison that negative people feed off the group's energy and lose that energy when one-on-one. Criticizing people in a group just makes them feel more embarrassed and resistant. It's an act of disrespect. See if the problems can be resolved amicably. If they are staff, you have leverage over them.

Use progressive discipline:

First offense. A one-on-one private warning/counseling.

Second offense. A written warning; cc your human resources officer and your board president.

Third offense. Punishment in proportion or dismissal, depending on the offense and history.

If the offense is more serious, you can skip steps. For example, if an employee is committing a crime, you can dismiss them immediately. Be fair and professional and include the human resources (HR) officer (and board president if you're dismissing a manager or longtime employee) in each step.

If a board member is negative, you may need the support of the president in the room to get the member to join the team. When dealing with board conflicts, always have another board member act as a mediator. Remember, they are your bosses. If you must sever the relationship, do so in a professional, above-board manner with the board of trustees in support. If you can't get that kind of support in the first hundred days, you will never get it. Nothing can be fixed without initial respect in your ability to do it. This time is when you will have the most leverage with the board. They want you to succeed, or they wouldn't have hired you. Use that leverage constructively.

8. Get Your Ideas to Become Their Ideas

Be prepared to hear people say to you after the inner circle meeting, "I have been telling people we should do this forever! I'm glad it's finally going to get done." Once you have heard this, you are on the right road. What they are subconsciously saying to you is, "I'm glad you acknowledged my ideas, and if we succeed, I'm going to know it was MY idea."

Once people believe the path is theirs and not yours, they are far more likely to be invested in it. When people take credit for the plan, you have succeeded.

Everyone has an ego, and until it's their idea, no one really wants to work on any plan. It has to be THEIR plan,
not yours. NEVER correct someone for taking credit of
your idea. That is a sure way to kill their participation
and enthusiasm. When people think it's their idea, you
are off to the races. You will always get your credit as the
leader. The best teams don't know they are being led.

9. Set Up the Stakeholders' Retreat

At the initial inner circle meeting, announce the need
for a key stakeholders' retreat to set the vision for the
organization's future. (See Chapter 6 on strategic planning.) Now you know what the problems are, who the
players are, and what their agendas and personalities
are. You have an idea how to fix the problems and set
the organization on the right path. Assign tasks to your
new team. Have board members generate enthusiasm
for the retreat by setting up the invite list. Have staff
handle the logistics. You will assign a staff person to
shepherd the needs assessment project (See Chapter 4).

The more you can get your team excited and busy
right from this meeting at implementing a strategy for
success, the more they will grow in respect and loyalty
for your leadership. Give everyone a role. Some may
suggest a role for themselves. Get excited about that. If
you aren't sure they can handle their roles, team them
with people who can. Leave no one out. Give them clear
and distinct deadlines for their tasks. This is crucial, both
to stay on time and to set the precedent that they will

be expected to meet deadlines with you in the lead. This holds them accountable.

10. Attitude Is Everything

The greatest thing a leader can do is have a great attitude. A good attitude by staff and stakeholders can double an organization's marketing efforts because everyone is talking about the breath of fresh air that started there. It can also double fundraising because those who contribute to your organization want to be with people who love their work and cheerfully carry out the mission.

If you are not a cheerful person by nature, do not become a leader of a non-profit (don't be a leader, period). If you are fighting polio, you don't want the leader of the organization to say, "We are never going to beat this thing." You don't want to hear him or her complain about the lack of funding or lack of staffing, either. None of those things makes you want to join or give money. You want to be part of something in which the leader is your best cheerleader. Your leader shouts, "We are going to beat this thing!"

We could be digging ditches, or working at a drive-through window, or something really horrible like working on Capitol Hill where nothing gets done. We have the most amazing jobs on earth. What we lack in big salaries, we make up for in job satisfaction. We make a difference every day. We sleep well at night knowing the world is a better place because we are in it. We are

supermen and women without the capes (tights are
optional). I feel as if I were the richest man in town.
And I never have to worry about what to do with all my
vacation time or my big corporate bonus. Those worries
are gone! I have always felt rich, whether I worked at
a shelter on skid row, a prison classroom, or a historic
mansion such as the cultural center I now run. When
someone's life changes in front of your eyes because of
your mission, no money can compare to that. And if
you come to work each day with that attitude, so will
your staff. If they can't, it might be time for new staff.
This has to be the number-one reason for success. Being
happy actually makes you happier. It's also the sexiest
quality for those of us not born looking like Brad Pitt or
Angelina Jolie. Happiness does make you better looking.

"I'm Fantastic"

I went to the funeral of a man who was the top real
estate agent in town for more than fifty years. His
grandson, Rob, who ran a successful winery in Napa,
told this story at the funeral: When he was fourteen, his
grandfather asked him how he was doing. Rob said, "I'm
not feeling too great today, Grandpa. My stomach hurts,
and my skateboard is busted." His grandfather took
him aside and said, "Robby, when people ask you how
you are, they really don't want to know how you are. If
you tell them something good, fine. But if you tell them
something bad, you are just going to bring them down,
and nobody wants to hang out with someone who is a

constant downer. So from now on, when someone asks you how you are, you say, 'Fantastic!' even if you aren't. And if you say you are fantastic, you eventually will be fantastic. You will make more friends that way." He said he never forgot the advice, and it was the best advice he ever got.

There is a tendency in non-profits to want to live in a state of constant crisis as a fundraising technique. But this becomes the boy who cried wolf. It will work once, but after a few times, people will cross the street when they see you coming so they don't have to talk to you. It's much better to be the successful non-profit everyone wants to be around because of the great positive feelings they get from being there. So next time someone asks how you are, say "Fantastic!" The next time people ask how things are going with your non-profit that you are rescuing from the brink of disaster, say, "Things were bad there for a while. I'm not going to lie. But now things are turning around, and we are getting back to our mission. Wait till you see what we are doing over there!"

Interviewing staff will give you a sense of the organization's culture, but it takes attitude to help you overcome that culture. If someone resists change, being negative and talking bad about you behind your back, don't worry. Don't follow that person. NEVER talk badly about anyone. I know this is hard to do. But gossip is a boomerang and always comes back around. If you stay upbeat and positive, they will lose the war. If you talk well of them while they run you down, others will take your side. The tide will turn toward you every time.

Eventually, you will prevail. Revolutions and hurricanes are destructive methods of change and often do not last. Nonviolent protests led by people like Mahatma Gandhi and Martin Luther King Jr. took longer but prevailed with lasting effects because they used positive attitudes against oppression to change opinion. Success comes from a happy heart and strong policies gathered through consensus.

A Mule for Inspiration

There is an old folk story about Mr. Johnson's prize mule. The mule was amazing and won every contest at the county fairs. This mule was known to save people from burning fires and push tractors off farmers stuck under them, and the stories go on and on. He was a legendary mule.

His neighbor, Farmer Jones, was jealous of that mule. One night he snuck into Mr. Johnson's barn and led that mule to his farm, where he had dug a ditch deep enough to cover up a prize mule and covered the pit in leaves and branches. When the mule walked on top of it, he fell into the hole. Farmer Jones started covering the hole as fast as he could with the intent of burying that prize mule alive. But every time the farmer threw a shovelful of dirt on that mule, he would just shake it all off, stomp it on down, and rise on up to a new level. This happened with each shovel: he would shake it all off, stomp it on down, and rise on up to a new level until he was standing over the covered pit. Since Farmer Jones had his back to the mule, he didn't see what was happening. And he didn't see when the mule kicked him in the fanny so hard that the farmer flew in the sky over the mountain ridge and was never seen or heard from again.

So when you feel things getting on you, trying to bury you alive, take a cue from a prize mule. You just shake it all off, stomp it on down, and rise on up to a new level! Your whole non-profit then can shake it all off, stomp it down, and rise on up to a new level.

Review

- You have one hundred days to prove yourself worthy. Don't let this time get by you. Hard work here will make the rest of your time easier.
- Leadership isn't giving orders. Ask people what direction they want to go and find consensus.
- You must have consensus to be successful. Ask people their opinions and listen.
- Decipher the code. Read between the lines of what the group says individually and translate it into the pressing problems for the group.
- Become an expert on your organization, its history, and how it's perceived in the community.
- Develop an inner circle among your staff and key stakeholders to be your think tank and key apostles of the organization.
- Fight pettiness with professionalism when negativity rears its ugly head. Don't fall into the trap of coming down to their level.

- Use progressive discipline when dealing with staff problems.
- Use a board member as a mediator when dealing with board problems.
- Ensure your ideas become the stakeholders' ideas is the goal. Let them own the ideas, even if it means swallowing your own ego to do it. When they are invested in their idea, it's more likely to get done.
- Set up a stakeholders' retreat with all the key personnel as soon as you have a handle on the organization and establish your inner circle.
- A positive attitude is everything.

Developing the Missionaries, Part I: Staff

Chapter 2

*In most cases being a good boss means hiring talented
people and then getting out of their way.*
—Tina Fey, "Bossypants"

T he culture of an organization is a key factor in
success and failure at this stage. A Negative Nelly
or a stick-in-the-mud can sink a growing organization
before it ever gets to sea. Egos can be used for positive
change. But egos can also block change. This is most
true among your staff. Your first twenty days sets the
tone for your office, which, in turn, sets the tone for
everything else. Therefore, getting the office in order is
your first order of business. While the last chapter dealt
with leadership, this chapter deals with supervision.
The two go hand in hand. Leadership is about going
first into the tunnel with the flashlight in a direction
your staff helps choose. Supervision is about making
sure everyone stays with you. Supervision is literally
defined as "looking" (vision) "over" (super). Supervision

isn't about consensus building but about mentorship—
training your staff to be the best and keeping up with
you in that tunnel. In the military they say, "We will
leave no man behind." That is supervision.

Staff members are the face of the organization on your
site and the face of programs that carry out your mission.
Staff problems can be the most visible ones but they are
also the easiest to solve because you have control over
your staff. It's common for a new leader to come into a
failing or stagnant organization to find a counterproduc-
tive staff culture. Some staff may have been there for
years and think they run the organization—they may
even have run it unofficially—but don't want to take
responsibility for the problems. They may want to keep
on running it. There may be staff wondering why you
were hired as director instead of them. Other staff may
be undertrained and doing their job poorly through no
fault of their own. Some staff may just have a bad attitude
or a personality conflict with you. They are too much like
you and have trouble toeing the line. You may have a staff
that whines and complains at every turn, or one who is
just negative about any change. You may have all of these
staff members in one office. That isn't to say that non-
profits have lousy staff—quite the contrary. Non-profit
staff members are usually dedicated individuals. But if
you are coming into an organization with problems—
which is why you were hired in the first place—expect
problems among the staff.

You do have a tool you can use with staff that you can't
use on other stakeholders: you are their boss. They report

directly to you. You evaluate their performance and have the power to dismiss or discipline them. It's tricky to find the balance between wanting to be liked as a leader and being strict as a boss. Ultimately best practices for raising children are also best practices for employees. (Some of these tips might also help with raising kids.)

Be Consistent

If you tell people no, do not turn around and recant because they complain. Don't let them do what you said they could not do, either. Make sure there is a process for complaints. Just like kids, they are testing you. If you give in after making a decision, they will know you can be easily manipulated.

Do Not Play Favorites

If you set up a policy for one employee, it should be the policy for all employees. Don't say no to one employee and yes to another. You can easily do this without knowing it and then wonder why an employee dislikes you. You could have a bad first impression of someone and disrespect him or her without realizing it. It's human nature to avoid people we don't enjoy being around. It's also normal to send out signals unconsciously. But your staff will pick up on this. If someone rubs you the wrong way, communicate with that person and try to get it straightened out in the beginning. It could be a misconception on your part that is driving a wedge and making for a bad situation. You can't worry about why someone may not like you, but you can make sure you are not the one driving the wedge and sabotaging yourself. My mentor in the prison system, Curtis Brown, used to say, "The best management training is the 'The Godfather' movies and books. Keep your friends close and your enemies closer." He was a great manager.

Never Yell at Employees or Discipline Them in Front of Others

Always take them to a private space to discipline one-on-one. We discussed this tenet in Chapter 1. Nothing is more disrespectful than berating someone in front of others. Someone may decide to do this to you, but remember that you are the leader. Doing it back to that person is no better than a parent throwing a tantrum because the child did it first. Be the adult in the situation. If you handle these situations professionally, your staff will respect you for it. When you are in a private space, never use foul language or blow your top. These things can be insulting and make you look unstable. Calm and cool is the rule. Out of control is the fool.

Have Reasonable Expectations and Deadlines

Never give an assignment without a deadline. If it's important, such as a grant or public communiqué, give an artificial deadline, so if it comes back incorrect, you have time to fix it. The bigger the project, the more time you must build into the schedule. Ask for it a week (or more) before you actually must have it.

I don't track my full-time staff's hours. I track their deadlines. They are all dedicated to the mission so I evaluate them on their ability to make meetings on time and meet deadlines with quality work. If they can do that, their hours are unimportant. The fact is they generally work more than forty hours because the office is attuned to the mission and tasks rather than the clock. I state my expectations clearly. If they miss more than two deadlines or meetings in a year, they will not be considered for staff bonuses or raises and could be dismissed from their work if missing the deadline was a significant problem to the organization. Three strikes and you're out. The strikes reset every year on their performance review. They do not like getting a strike! This breeds an air of pride in work. I model the behavior I want from my staff. I give myself strikes and get mad at myself when I make a mistake. Approximately once a year I make a huge goof. I joke that two more and I will need to fire myself. I tell them they will have to get the board to fire me.

One time the staff and I were moving something out of my office, and I leaned a historic door against another door. When the other door opened, the historic door fell, shattering a leaded glass mirror into a thousand pieces. I wanted to crawl under the carpet. These glass mirrors are not made as they used to be. We all make dumb mistakes, but hopefully not too often or too big.

My staff could tell how upset I was at myself. That kind of pride in work and horror in failure is modeled.

Expect Quality Work

Set your standards high, and the staff will follow suit. If something is subpar, let them know in a constructive way. Make them redo it. You must do quality work to be thought of as a quality organization. Better to have staff complain about your high standards than to have none. That is a sign of respect.

Set and Distribute Policies

It's best to create, document, and distribute blanket policies for issues that affect the entire organization. For example, someone may ask to leave early during a program, and you say no. This person is upset because another employee got off early last week during a program. But he or she doesn't realize that the other employee was the bookkeeper and had no responsibility during the program, while the one who is upset is in charge of hospitality. You can avoid this in the future by releasing a memo on the policy for excused absences on program days. The policy would spell out what the rules are, who can leave and when. The memo will also show why the other employee was excused and show that it wasn't a personal attack on anyone. Any time a new issue comes up and seems as if it may recur, I weigh all the options, discuss it with staff, get consensus, decide how it fits with the mission (LMV), make a decision, and release a memo with that decision as a new policy. This way everyone knows that the decision is what will be done from now on.

An example from my life is locking doors. When I started at the Muck, staff members were forgetting to close and lock doors consistently. It was not only a security issue but a safety problem. People were wandering in after hours. In a former job, a staff member forgot to lock the center one night, and a man used the center to rape a girl who was playing in the park outside. I took this very seriously. I sent out a policy memo that anyone who forgets to lock doors or set alarms would get a strike. If they did it three times in a year, they would be dismissed or lose their key privileges. I cited the rape incident. After that, doors were locked consistently. No more problems.

Have Employees Sign a Contract

The contract is a set of rules or the last page of an employee handbook. By signing the contract, they acknowledge that they have read the rules and will abide by them. Every year it's updated with new policies, and made available as a hard copy and online to all staff. Now no one can say, "I didn't know what the rule was" or "You never told us that." The employee handbook should have employment information that is standard in employee handbooks, like definitions of employment, benefits, grievance procedures, discipline procedures, and rules. There are many templates for these items online and with other peer organizations. New policy memos are added every year to the employee handbook.

Have Annual Performance Reviews

Make sure the employees know they are being reviewed. You should review a new employee in the first three or six months, after a probationary period. There are many effective formats for this. They should also have a chance to review themselves.

At the Muck, we use a survey format that Human Resources distributes to the employee and his or her supervisor automatically the week before the employee's employment anniversary. (We use Survey Monkey; www.surveymonkey.com.) The employee and supervisor rate the employee on things like timeliness; making deadlines; relationships with staff, patrons and supervisor; quality of work; quantity of work; and so on. The finished surveys are sent to the supervisor so he or she can see how the employee rated himself or herself versus what the supervisor rated. The surprising thing is that even on bad performance reviews, employees often will rate themselves lower than the supervisors.

A meeting is scheduled on the employee's work anniversary. The employee and the supervisor discuss the review, agree on what needs to be improved, and set goals for the coming year. A good review might result in bonuses, salary raises, promotions, and/or awards. Bad reviews might result in probation, a salary freeze, a cut in hours, or dismissal. Many employees will be in between.

Obviously in non-profits we can't afford to give bonuses, salary raises, and promotions to everyone who deserves it each year. As a field, we generally have amazing employees who work well above and beyond the call of duty. What we can do is give appreciation lunches, awards, more prestigious titles, vacation time, training, plum assignments, and trips to conferences as rewards. In surveys of what employees think of as most important incentives for working, money never comes in first.[1] It's usually around 6 or 7 out of 10. Respect is always first. So any way you can show employees you respect them will mean more than a raise, providing the employees are already reasonably compensated for what they do. A $1,000 raise in a year works out to approximately $26 per pay period after taxes. That isn't going to get people to continue their hard work as much as a public award or even a nice lunch on the boss with a thank-you. If they know you are trying to help them get more knowledge, training, titles, and experience that will lead to them moving up the ladder, they will be happy.

Set Them Free

Don't have the attitude that good staff must stay with you forever. If you are a good mentor, you are groom-

---

1   *There are hundreds of these surveys, and "more pay" usually comes in between number 5 and 7 out of 10. (http://blog.sparkhire. com/2012/07/07/workplace-incentives-what-do-employees-really -want-infographic/).*

ing them for better things, and you will be happy when they leave you to move up, provided they have been with you long enough to justify the training you have invested into them. If an employee has been with you two to three years or more and gets a great opportunity for a promotion, don't begrudge the employee a shot. You may end up as peers and partners later, and that person will never forget your mentorship and leadership.

When I was younger working in government, I was up for a big promotion and didn't get it. When I asked why, I was told that I was too valuable where I was to be moved. Were they telling me someone not as good as I was got the promotion because that other person was not as valuable and could be moved? I was told, "Yes, in fact. We needed to move someone and couldn't fire her, so we promoted her." I resigned a few weeks later. So they ended up losing me anyway.

I have many former employees who still call me for advice and help. Some I worked with more than ten years ago. Some partner with me, as they are now directors. I enjoy these relationships. I am proud to see people I mentored become successful.

From an organizational standpoint, it's not good to have a stagnant staff. It's good for staff to change over time. New blood brings new ideas and new opportunities. It's the same for directors. An organization grows from a regular and controlled influx of new blood. An organization is like a human body—every seven years it has completely regenerated itself with new cells. In an organization it should be approximately seven to nine

years. Approximately every nine years the organization
should be renewed. This is why board terms usually
are limited to three three-year cycles. This is similar to
why presidents are limited to two four-year terms. This
doesn't mean you must leave your job in nine years.
A sabbatical, new board leadership, or other ways to
rejuvenate the soul might be in order. If you start a big
capital project that takes fifteen years to complete, you
want to see it to fruition. Just find ways to rejuvenate
and keep it fresh along the way.

Use Progressive Discipline

Don't be afraid to discipline your staff. Staff, like children, will take advantage of an authority figure who uses
no authority and lets them run wild. See Chapter 1 for
more details on progressive discipline.

Reward and Train Your Staff

In our office rewards go hand-in-hand with training.
Most staff members want to move up in the world. Each
of our Muck staff receives a $400 yearly stipend to be
used toward approved training or conferences. This is a
benefit of employment. If they don't get training, they
lose the money. We also take a quarterly field trip to a
like-minded non-profit. We visit other cultural centers
or historical sites that are similar to us in mission, organization size, or budget. Then we invite their staff to visit
us. This has been the most productive training we do.

Staff can compare notes with their counterparts. We get ideas from them we can implement to make us better. We can see where we are in our development compared to our peers. I view it as a team-building exercise, and we have great discussions over lunch during these field trips. The staff used to dread these field trips when we started them because they had to drop their work for a whole day. But soon they enjoyed the experience and the break. Now they complain if one has to be postponed or delayed. They want more of them.

We also hold an annual staff training retreat on things that must be taught: first aid/CPR, management, supervision of interns, harassment, diversity training, emergency plans, and so on. We provide lunch and a party after the retreat. Sometimes we do this away from our work. Getting away from work reframes and relaxes the training and those being trained. Staff members are more open when in a beautiful setting that isn't work. Sometimes a board member will donate a cabin in the mountains for the training, or we will use a public park space.

We provide a monthly birthday lunch where we treat people who have birthdays in that month, and the rest pay their own way. We have had staff-generated get-togethers such as dinners, parties, and bowling nights once each month as well. Every year at the annual retreat, I give the staff a book that I feel will help them grow (I got this idea from reading about Phil Jackson, former coach of the Los Angeles Lakers. He used this book as a way to cement his goals for the individual player). We also do a staff-generated fundraiser for the organization every three to six months. This is a team-building exercise, but it also brings home the point that we are all invested in the mission. All these things have created a culture of fun and family while keeping the emphasis on the mission.

The Delegation Speech

Another important aspect of developing a positive, conducive culture is defining the word "delegation." In my first hundred days, I gather the managers—my inner circle—and ask them to define delegation (I give this talk to new managers also when they come in). Many people think delegation means giving a subordinate things you don't want to do, so you can do the important stuff. But that is wrong. A "delegate" is someone a leader sends to represent him or her in an important function. I tell the managers they are delegates. Delegation empowers someone to act on your behalf with all the powers of your office. I expect them, as managers, to be experts in their field and constantly update their training and knowledge. I depend on them to know things in their field better than I do because they are my experts. I do not do the work myself, or redo their work. They are my brain trust. I expect them to do quality work on time as I would do it because they are my delegates. And when I send them out into the community, I expect them to act as me—my delegate. I also expect them to train those working under them to do the same.

After I give them this talk, the staff feel the importance of their office, the weight of responsibility, and
the respect and appreciation I have for them. Giving
staff this kind of authority makes them better, more
responsible, and more committed. Not having to micro-
manage staff allows me to spend time on my own work.
Everyone is happy. If you have staff whom you feel can't
be your delegates, you might have the wrong staff in the
wrong positions for growth.

Staff Spectrum

Among your staff, the spectrum of experiences ranges
from highly trained staff (at a higher salary who are
already set in their ways) to untrained staff with great
skills (whom you can mold the way you want them
to be). The former hit the ground running and can do
things quickly but must learn your style. They might
also have established bad habits or habits that don't
work for you. The latter can become great but require
much time to train. Train them well and they will be
great. But they can also take all their training and leave
you for another gig. The best office is a balance of
people all along the spectrum. Both have their positives
and negatives, but it's important to recognize where
staff are on this spectrum and determine if they need
more training and hand-holding, or if they need more
help adapting to your style.

People you hire or promote are generally going to
be more loyal to you than people you inherit when you

start. So the first hundred days is an important time to get your staff in order. If someone is a problem and not coming around, get rid of that person sooner rather than later, when he or she may have affected others and your honeymoon period is wearing off. If the opportunity presents itself to hire new staff or reorganize the office, take great care in doing this and be very involved, as the staff you hire can set the tone for the office. Use temps when needed so you don't have to rush this process. When hiring, attitude should be as high a priority as skill set. A skilled employee with a bad attitude—or worse, a bland attitude—can undermine your whole process.

Contractor Versus Employee

It's also important to look at contract labor versus salaried staff. Some contractor jobs would be done more efficiently with paid staff. In other cases, it might be the reverse. The main factors in determining this is the scope of work, importance to your mission, and cost. Contractors cost more by the hour but do a specific job well without your having to pay a salary and benefits. Salaried employees are cheaper by the hour but require more in a regular schedule, benefits, and legal responsibilities on your part and process.

For example, say your organization is an after-school program for soccer. You employ a full-time janitor when the program only runs from 4 p.m. to 7 p.m. Is janitorial core to the mission? Is the cost too high for a

full-time salary plus benefits? Can it be done in a few
hours after work by a contracted crew? If so, switch to
a contractor.

In another case, you may have a program contractor who runs your soccer camp at $30 per hour for
four hours after school daily. But he gets paid another
stipend to manage the other contractors, drive the van,
and deal with problems from parents and is working
twenty-nine hours per week (the legal maximum) at
$30 per hour. He lost his other day job. You could of-
fer him a full-time managerial job at $18 an hour plus
benefits. You will end up paying several thousand more
each year for him, but you will get eleven extra hours
each week and more commitment on his part. He will
make more money in the long run doing what he loves
and have a career path and health benefits for his family.
You will get a lot more for your money and get a great
new manager without paying a lot extra for it.

At the Muck we had a contract gardener we turned
into a staff position because with almost nine acres of
grounds, we got more bang for the buck with a staff
employee, but we changed the bookkeeper position to
contract, which allowed us to hire more needed staff
and have more eyes on the books to double-check
them. These changes were part of a revamp that helped
double our budget and staffing.

When deciding on these issues, ask yourself, "Does it
help the mission? Does it save money or spend it more
wisely? Does it increase the scope of work for the cost?"
This is smart management.

Review

- Be consistent with all employees regardless of your feelings about them.
- Make decisions as a matter of policy, not as a matter of playing favorites.
- Never yell at employees or discipline them in front of others.
- Have reasonable expectations and deadlines.
- Expect and demand quality work from all employees and yourself.
- Set policies for things that come up rather than make your decisions on a case-by-case basis.
- Have employees sign a contract stating what is expected of them.
- Have annual performance reviews for your staff and expect your board to evaluate you.
- Don't get precious about your employees. Help them in their career path even if it means losing a good employee. Change is good.
- If people perform well, reward them. Rewards don't have to be expensive. It comes down to training them and showing them respect.
- If people perform poorly, use progressive discipline.
- Teach staff the principle of delegation and empower them to take responsibility for their jobs.
- Expect a diversity of workers, from highly skilled to new employees, and from contract to salaried staff. Know the benefits and drawbacks of each.

Now that you have set the mood by getting everyone
on board in consensus, determining the non-profit culture at your organization and all the politics that implies,
and setting a great attitude example for stakeholders,
you are ready to examine the most important part of
changing your culture and everything else: the mission.

The Mission Statement

Chapter 3

What if NASA's mission was ambiguous?

Have It Your Way.

—Burger King

The mission statement is everything. If the organization's mission statement doesn't engage the staff, board, volunteers, and community with passion and direction, nothing can grow or change. If your organization's culture is out of whack, chances are your stakeholders have lost touch with the mission. If you've lost touch with your stakeholders, you have lost touch with your mission. If you never could get any stakeholders, your mission statement might be weak. No amount of leadership and attitude will help if your mission statement isn't compelling at the start.

This would mean that you might not have a real reason to exist. You must show that your mission statement is unique to the field in which you are playing. You must frame your mission statement correctly. If you are trying to start a non-profit organization to cure a rare disease that affects on average three people in the United States each year, other than the family members of the three people who died, who is going to care? What makes your mission compelling in the face of so many other more debilitating diseases like cancer? Now if you tell me that disease is polio, and if not cured it could make a comeback and kill millions worldwide, then it becomes much more crucial. Everything comes down to how you frame your mission.

You spent your first twenty days creating and leading a team while discovering your organization and its mission. You have set up a stakeholders' retreat to create the organizational vision in ten to twenty days. While your staff gets ready for that retreat, you must assess the mission and how it's framed.

What Is a Mission Statement?

A mission statement is the bumper sticker that sums up why you exist. It's the reply you give in elevators when people ask what you do as a non-profit. It's the several words or sentences that make people care and want to help. Who are we? "We take care of people in war or after a disaster." "We are looking to prevent and cure cancer." These are fine for a large national or international organization. But a local non-profit needs more detail. It could be "We provide after-school soccer programs in Tampa Bay, Florida," or "We help autistic kids through horseback riding therapy in Burbank, California."

A mission statement should be brief and provide some

detail and measurable objectives. Does this mission statement reflect us? Is it compelling? Is it measurable? It will
not be "to create world peace." A small non-profit's objective is usually confined to a geographic region. "We want
to help all the teens in the greater Omaha area do X." With
this, you can measure whether you reach those teens.

Great examples of this can be found in corporate
mission statements, which often get translated to com-
mercial taglines. My favorite example is Burger King.
When the restaurant chain came out in the 1960s, they
were contenders with McDonald's, who became famous
for delivering fast food with consistent quality. Burger
King wanted to take it one step further. The golden
arches are fast because they only have one way to do
their burgers—on an assembly line. Burger King burgers
would be done just as fast but made to order. You could
"Have It Your Way." That was their mission. Consistent,
quality fast food, made to order. You can measure
whether customers are having it their way. They became
the number-two fast-food chain in the world in no time.

What is the non-profit version of this? Let's look
at Make-A-Wish Foundation's mission statement:
"We grant wishes to children with life-threatening
medical conditions." Who doesn't want to be the fairy
godmother or father? Boys & Girls Clubs' mission is to
"enable young people, especially those most in need,
to reach their full potential as productive, responsible,
caring citizens." Who doesn't want to help with that? It
allows them to measure a broad scope of things, from
sports to computers to tutoring.

Assessing Community Need

The essence of non-profit leadership is in making the
community feel the need and the mission after the crisis
no longer feels urgent. If someone else in your area is
accomplishing this mission already, you don't need to
exist, so make sure your mission is specific enough to
matter. If you are a dance program in a city full of dance
programs, what sets you apart in addressing community needs that the others do not? If you can't answer
this question, you might need to merge with a similar
organization or not exist at all.

Missions come from need and usually from crisis.
Medical non-profits usually start after many people die
from a disease epidemic and the community of people
who lost them band together. Some non-profits come
from war. The Red Cross started after the Civil War.
Others come from tragedy or natural disasters, like the
1992 Los Angeles riots and Hurricane Katrina, to address
a need. But how do you keep up the energy when the
riots are twenty years behind us or the initial devasta-
tion of Katrina is long past? How do you keep the fire
burning to cure and prevent AIDS when medicines
make it possible to live with AIDS? These are the arenas
of a great non-profit leader. It starts with a great mission
statement and a commitment to that mission.

The Needs Assessment Tool

How do you lead a staff when you have no previous
connection to the mission, but they do? Conversely, if

you are connected to your mission but the staff members are not, how do you plug them in?

Your prime directive is to connect the community and staff to the mission. A great mission statement begins with a needs assessment. You will use this tool as part of your strategic plan, in grants you write, and in selling potential investors to your cause.

A needs assessment includes four things:

1. A theory of change
2. Negative factors
3. Positive factors
4. Outcomes

Theory of Change

The theory of change is similar and can be identical to your mission statement. Your theory is that by this mission you are changing the community for the better. Now we are going to prove it by documenting negative factors before your existence, positive experiences and testimonials afterward, and showcasing these outcomes to the community. For example, if your organization is to provide after-school sports programs to kids, your theory of change states that by providing these programs, kids will become better citizens and avoid crime, drugs, and negative influences.

Negative Factors

You can document negative contributing factors in the community: broken and single-parent homes, latchkey

kids, poverty, gangs, drug abuse, peer pressure that
frowns on education. You can get statistics on these
factors usually from United Way reports, police reports,
press reports, and so on. You can easily document that
X percent lives in poverty; there were X number of gang
arrests of juveniles last year; that juvenile arrests are
trending up or down; and so on. You want a statisti-
cal snapshot of the problem you are addressing. Most
communities have an annual "State of the Community"
report that shows all these statistics. A medical non-
profit might look at smoking, eating habits, and lack of
exercise as contributing factors that can be documented
with studies and reports.

Positive Factors

You can then identify positive factors of change caused
by your organization such as male role models, tutoring,
positive peer pressure, leadership training, incentives
to do well in school, and the moral compass one gets
from sports and teamwork. You can research these
factors and show statistics that prove them to address
the problems of the negative factors, such as the Office
of Juvenile Justice & Delinquency Prevention statistics,
which proves that the vast majority of all juvenile crime
takes place between 3 p.m. to 7 p.m. You can show
that the Boston Model from the mid-1980s showed
that when the worst juvenile gang leaders were locked
up and after-school programs increased significantly,
violent juvenile crime dropped significantly (this is
known across the country as "Weed & Seed"). A com-

pendium of research on this exists. The same is true of almost anything for which there is a non-profit. There is a compendium of research on the affect of arts, the importance of drug research on disease, the diversity of homelessness and ways they can be helped, and so on.

Outcomes

Once you show the negative background and the positive consequences of your non-profit, you can show the outcomes that should/do happen with your non-profit being there. These are the actual statistics of what you have done in this community. This takes it from a national statistic to a local statistic because of your intervention. For example: "Since our sports non-profit has come in three years ago, juvenile crime has fallen by 40 percent." You can also give actual individual anecdotes. "Johnny Smith was arrested three times and sent to juvenile hall before coming to our programs. He was running with the local gang and experimenting with drugs. Since coming to our program, he is the captain of the football team, his grades went from Fs to As, and he is looking at colleges on scholarship. He received the leadership award from the city last year. Johnny says, 'I owe my life to these people. I would be dead or in jail if not for them.'"

Compelling statistics and testimonials are exactly what you need to revitalize stakeholders, investors, and the community to the importance of your mission. These make you relevant again and push you to the front of the line when people are considering what charities to reward with funding. Investors want more than the feel-ing they are doing good. They want proof. Once you get these statistics and testimonials out into the community through multiple sources and stakeholders, you will no longer be begging them to help. They will be asking you how they can help. The whole dynamic of fundraising has changed. Once investors ask you for help, it's now their idea and they now have ownership of your mission. The sky is the limit to what they will do for you.

Hard Data and Investor Relationships

It would be fine if you could tell a potential investor, "We hold sports programs after school and think they are helpful." But how much more effective would it be to tell a potential investor, "Did you know most juvenile crime is perpetrated by youth on other youth between 3 and 7 p.m.? There is a compendium of research show-ing that when our sports programs run, juvenile crime drops by more than 40 percent. Programs like this make our community safer for your children." Now you are fortified with knowledge, statistics, and energy that make your mission important and crucial again. You can check out the local police statistics and keep your own on how your community fares against a commu-nity nearby that doesn't have this kind of non-profit. This might even lead to expansion of your non-profit or mentoring a neighboring community to start its own.

Nothing is more powerful than statistics and hard data in terms of driving home the power of the mission.

Once you are armed with your needs assessment showing that you are needed in your community, the mission
statement wording becomes more apparent.

Review

- Understand the mission statement as a bumper
  sticker that sums up why you exist.
- Conduct a needs assessment with:
  a. A theory of change
  b. Negative factors
  c. Positive factors
  d. Outcomes
- Be able to provide potential investors with hard data
  on the importance of your mission and your ability
  to serve your community.

You can start your mission statement during your inner-
circle meeting and develop it at the beginning of your
strategic planning retreat. Nothing else can be done until
this has been defined and agreed upon by consensus.
The work your staff does researching the needs assessment will also bring them into focus on the importance
of the mission statement and how the needs assessment
translates to funding for the mission. Each of these steps
in the first hundred days solidifies you as a leader who
makes substantial change by redefining the organization
through a revitalization of the mission. Now you are ready
to redefine the board through the prism of the mission.

Developing the Missionaries, Part II:
Board and Volunteers

Chapter 4

When torrential water tosses boulders it is because of momentum. When the strike of a hawk breaks the body of its prey, it is because of timing.

—Sun Tzu, "The Art of War"

Successful non-profits understand momentum and timing. This is never more true than in managing the board of directors. Sun Tzu also says that for an army to be successful, those in power must allow their generals the freedom to manage the war. For you to be effective, you need a supportive board of trustees who don't interfere with the day-to-day operations of the mission but provide the force you need to fight the good fight. In addition to staff, it will be your board and volunteers who carry out your mission in the community. They are the primary catalysts for growth.

As you enter into the stakeholders' retreat and set goals for the organization, you must understand your

board, their deficiencies, and their strengths. You can't
do that until you understand what makes a board effective and their role. You aren't expected to change
the board in your first hundred days. But by your first
forty days, you should know your board. You can start
training your board to work in a way that is conducive
to mission building. As Sun Tzu says, "Management of
the many is the same as management of the few; it's all a
matter of organization."

Theoretically, it's not your job to change the board.
They are your bosses. They hired and monitor you.
Realistically, though, the board is made up of volunteers with other full-time jobs and priorities. You are
the leader of the organization and must develop the
most effective board possible. How do you accomplish
that? There is a great line by Lainie Kazan, who plays
the wife in the movie *My Big Fat Greek Wedding*. She
says, "The men may be the head of the house, but the
women are the neck, and the neck can turn the head
anyway it wants!" You train the board to be the board
you want. The board is the head of the organization;
you are the neck.

Board Relations

The effectiveness of the board is one of the biggest
reasons a non-profit moves from a mid-sized to a large
non-profit. A small non-profit can be very successful
with a good leader and an ineffective board. A mid-sized
non-profit can be successful with a good leader and a

mid-functioning board. But to move beyond takes a very effective leader and board.

The Three *T*s: Time, Talent, and Treasure

What makes a board effective? An effective board has an even divide of the three *T*s: time, talent, and treasure.

One-third of the board should comprise people with the time to share their passion for the mission and who want to help. These might be younger retirees or alumni of your programs or their parents. They may not have a great deal of money, but they make up for it in volunteerism. They are the legs and arms of the board and do all the heavy lifting for busier board members. They generally also have great wisdom separating them from a normal volunteer and make you say, "You should be on the board." If you don't have these people, staff members do all the legwork, and the board will distract the staff from the mission and programs.

Another third of the board should have special talents that you need and for which you would have to pay if they were not on the board, such as accountants, lawyers, web designers, printers, marketing people, social butterflies, fundraisers, or publicists. These are all valuable and expensive things you use quite often; advice and in-kind service of this nature is invaluable. Notice I put social butterfly on the list. This is a very important board position. Much investment in the mission comes by word of mouth through parties with their many friends. Do not underestimate this skill.

The final third are people who have money or access
to money—treasure. They might be a vice president at
a bank, have a family foundation, or play golf with business leaders. Notice I didn't say they all had to be rich.
Someone who is a good salesman with rich friends can
sometimes get more investors than a rich person who
isn't social.

Board of Trustees, Not Directors

An effective board is also designed on a non-profit—
not a business—model. Many board members come
from the business world and have ideas that your organization should run like a business in which fundraising
is the number-one priority. An effective board realizes
that they are not a corporate "board of directors" looking for the bottom line. They are a "board of trustees."
The difference is that a board of trustees doesn't
"direct" but is entrusted with a mission; the bottom
line isn't financial but community-minded. An effective
board of trustees doesn't ask about profit. Rather, they
should consider:

- How many people used our services?
- How many programs did we do?
- Did we reach the goals for our mission?

These things are not necessarily the same as profit,
as goals can be reached in organizations without money
being part of the equation.

Jeffrey Wilcox, CFRE, at Third Sector Company and my trainer at Executive Service Corps., used a solar system as the model for an organizational chart rather than the typical hierarchical chart of board-over-CEO-over-staff. In his chart the sun was the mission. The board and CEO orbit the mission most closely, protecting it. Around them are the staff and key volunteers. In the next ring are investors and clients. Beyond that ring are former alumni of the programs and former investors. And in the outermost ring is the community at large. In this way, the non-profit's organizational chart is part of the mission. The chart shows that people are not hierarchical, but driven by the mission. And the people closest to the mission have the job of bringing people in the outer circles closer to the mission. If your board

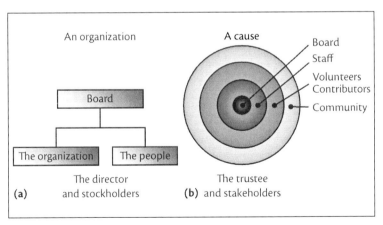

Figure 1. (a) Corporate organization vs. (b) non-profits. (Source: Jeffrey Wilcox; used with permission.)

can grasp this concept and carry out the mission as the bottom line, they will be more effective.

Term Limits

Another component of effective boards is length of service and the way in which they transition. Ineffective boards will have members, often very good people, on their boards for twenty years or more. There comes a point at which they are no longer effective and are burned out. People brag, "I've served on this board for twenty years." Usually that interprets to "this organization has stagnated for most of twenty years." If they were effective, they would have a plan in place to build the organization to the top of their ability and then provide for an infusion of new blood with new ideas and abilities who would grow it more.

Effective boards usually have in their bylaws a term of three years and a limit of three terms, for a total of nine years that someone can serve. Many organizations have this but don't enforce it. You have the opportunity to do so. Remind them that if they don't follow their own bylaws and someone sues the non-profit, they will be personally liable, and the directors and officers (D&O) insurance you pay may not cover them.[1] That will get their knickers in a twist.

---

1   Generally, if someone sues the board, that person can sue the board members personally and individually, and they would not be covered by D&O insurance.

Most boards ignore their bylaws because they don't have anyone viable who can take their place. That is where process comes into play. They don't have anyone viable because they have no process for succession. If I had a dime for every time a board president or committee chair told me, "I would love to step down, but I just can't find anyone dumb enough to take my place," I would be a wealthy man.

An effective board creates a recruitment committee that works with the executive director to bring in new board members every year. This committee identifies great and diverse new board members who reflect the community and the needs of the Three *T*s. The terms are staggered so new board members are not recruited all at once. In effective boards, officers are also recruited to replace outgoing officers. The president is aided by a past president and an incoming president. The past president is the institutional memory and can help train the incoming president with strategic planning and advice. The incoming president would run the recruitment committee to shape the future board with whom he'll work. Effective boards have a president for a three-year term. An effective president may be reelected to a second term but would want to groom someone at that point. An effective board plans and implements this vision of the future.

Some Misconceptions about Boards of Trustees

A board's main priority is to ensure that the mission

is accomplished and that it's a rewarding experience. You meet people from all walks of life, and you develop networks and lifelong friends (many people join boards for this reason). Fighting for a cause together creates a bond similar to what soldiers feel for their units. For people who don't exactly love their jobs, board service can bring much meaning and joy to their lives. There are, however, some basic misconceptions:

"Their main job is fundraising."

Fundraising is one function of the board. However, board members are responsible for the following:

- Oversight of the executive director
- Succession planning and recruitment
- Fundraising, endowment, and development
- Strategic planning and vision (with the executive director)
- Oversight of accounting practices and accounts
- Infrastructure

Infrastructure means ensuring that the physical organization is in order. This might mean developing a capital campaign for a new building, helping secure needed space, or just assuring that the CEO has resources to repair and replace things when needed.

Fundraising in this sense isn't about board members going out and shaking down their friends to the point where the friends crouch down behind the sofa and pretend they are not home when the board member comes knocking. This isn't effective. We will discuss this more in Chapter 7, but primarily these board members get others involved with the mission and let them make their own decisions about the checkbook. That is a much easier sell. If you are connecting people to your favorite charity, you are just sharing with them what makes you feel good. Asking them to help with a fundraising event, or to tutor kids after school, or to visit kids in the hospital, or whatever your organization does—this isn't hard because you believe in it. You know firsthand of the transformative powers of helping others in your organization.

"Being on boards is for people with money."

Some of the best board members with whom I have worked did not have money. When I was running a theatre company in juvenile halls, a sixteen-year-old read an article about us in the newspaper and wanted to hold a fundraiser for us at her school. I was touched and agreed. I didn't realize that her school was one of the most prestigious private high schools in the county of Los Angeles. Her classmates were the children of celebrities and power brokers. She raised more than $8,000 with a talent show. Denzel Washington was in the audience, Jason Alexander and Seth Greene were judges. It was unreal. I asked the board to invite her to be on our board. They laughed until they realized I was serious. She joined and had better access to people we wanted than anyone else on the board. When she graduated I wrote a support letter for her, and she received a national Coca-Cola scholarship. We helped each other out. It was a great example of why looking at a board member as a pocketbook is a bad idea. I have had boards that included welfare parents (whose kids were in our programs). They were great board members because they acted as unpaid staff.

Even though board members don't have to be rich, they must understand they have responsibilities to invest in the organization. Some boards have a threshold of board dues that would keep moderate-income people out. I am a proponent of board dues. However, if the key is getting them to invest, offer an alternative to a straight financial donation: a "give or get" principle and an in-kind stipulation. In other words, you can tell prospective board members that they have an obligation to give $250 yearly in board dues. But that could be done with in-kind services or even volunteer hours for those who can't afford the money. This brings home the idea that we are about serving the mission, not raising money.

Another way for board members to invest is to have them promise to leave part of their estate to the organization. It could be a threshold of 10 percent or $10,000. If they do not have a great estate, they can still leave 10 percent. Someone can leave stock or a time-share to the organization. Should something happen, it could become a significant gift in that person's name to an organization he or she loved. If people add in their will that they want money—in lieu of flowers—to go to the organization with 10 percent of the estate to start a new endowment, it could remake the organization's future. When someone gives a onetime gift of $10,000, it funds a great program for a year and then it's gone. But when someone leaves an endowment gift of $10,000, the organization gets approximately 5 percent, or $500, forever. Forever! Multiply that by a hundred gifts over the years, and soon the organization has an income stream to cover its operations forever.

Our largest endowment at the Muck did not come from a rich person. Jane Deming, a single music teacher for more than fifty years, bought her home when Fullerton still consisted of orange groves and orchards. When she passed away, she gave her home to start two endowments, one for us and one for music programs in the city. Her home was worth more than $1 million. Now every year, music programs happen citywide under the Jane Deming Endowment in perpetuity.

"Boards are time-consuming."

Effective boards of trustees would differ with this. In effective boards, they meet monthly or quarterly for two hours or less. You are generally required to serve on a committee that meets on your schedule once a month for a couple hours. The work you do for the committee is generally part of your job, so it doesn't take additional personal time. For example, if you are the board attorney or accountant or web guru, you would be doing these things as part of your work. It would be the company's contribution to the community. If you are the social butterfly or board recruiter, you would simply be talking about the organization in the normal course of your interactions with friends and doing your normal activities. Therefore the commitment of your personal time is a few hours each month for meetings and touching base. The real commitment is in making the mission a priority in your life.

"I'm not important enough to serve."

If you have time, talent, or treasure, you are important to a board. If you really care about an organization, it's your obligation to serve. They need apostles to spread the gospel. They need workers to supplement staff. They need help.

Board commitment shouldn't be done for status, corporate ladder climbing, networking, or any other reason that pertains to making your social situation better. Board membership is about an intense passion for an issue that drives you to get involved.

- "My mother died of Alzheimer's, so I will get involved with a local charity that works with patients."
- "My son was killed in gang violence, so I will work with an after-school program to stem the tide of gangs in our community."
- "I took a class in ceramics and it changed my life, so I want to serve our local cultural center."

These are all common stories. It's about fighting the things that affect you negatively or giving back to the things that strengthened you.

Don't Discount the Volunteers

Board members are volunteers, but there are, I hope, many more volunteers at your organization. This is the pool of people from which you will draw your board members. It's the staff's responsibility to recruit and maintain volunteers. Volunteers may make up committees that do a specific task like host a fundraiser, help with a program, help maintain the facility, and so on. They also could be:

- Student interns
- Program aides
- Developmentally disabled groups
- Senior groups
- High school leadership groups
- Event staff pulled from various volunteer organizations in your community

Each can help with a specific need, including but not limited to mailings, fundraising peer-to-peer, thrift or gift shop management, or docent programs.

At the Muck, we use all these groups in our cultural center and host more than six hundred volunteers each year. Two hundred serve on two different fundraising committees: a senior women's group runs our gift shop, provides docents, runs concessions, and holds its own fundraisers; and a mostly men's group puts on an annual car show fundraiser. Altogether, these groups raise more than $50,000 net for the organization. Sixty volunteers are student interns who design our marketing material;

work in the office with grants, databases, and correspondence; help as event staff; or work as classroom aides. Twenty volunteers come from a developmentally disabled school to clean before our weekly concerts. The rest of our volunteers help with eighty individual events each year coming from local high schools, Boys & Girls Clubs, Scouts, church groups, senior centers, and volunteer groups like National Charity League, One Stop Centers, and the Volunteer Center. Some events require as many as 120 volunteers at a time.

How did we get so many? Word of mouth. They have doubled since my tenure. We recruit through our resource map (which we will discuss shortly). Once people enjoy their experience, they spread the word, and before long you have a wait list of volunteers. We have some who sign up for three months and stay for over a year.

Treat your volunteers with respect and reward them for good behavior; discipline them like staff otherwise. This is the secret to building a great reputation for getting and maintaining volunteers. Most volunteers think of themselves as staff if they become close to the organization. It makes sense then to deal with them as staff and hold them accountable accordingly. Regular volunteers in our center get invited to staff field trips, chamber lunches, appreciation lunches, and birthday lunches with staff. A representative of each of our two major committees sits on our board as an ex-officio member of the board. Our interns receive reference letters, and we forward job postings to them. We have hired several and recommended others to other jobs.

We have placed at least a dozen interns in well-paying jobs in their fields.

Food is the best incentive for volunteers. For the small cost of treating people to a lunch now and then, we get so much in a trained labor force that doubles our staffing abilities. They consider themselves part of the group, and they are.

Several volunteers came to us as disgruntled volunteers from other non-profits with horror stories of how they were treated in other places. Some managers treat their volunteers as slave labor with the attitude, "you are free labor, so you must not be worth much." It's amazing how long some people will hang out in a non-profit that treats them badly because they care so much about the mission. These are the people you want. Why wouldn't you treat them as well as you would a major investor who gives your organization thousands? Don't these volunteers do thousands of dollars of free labor for you without a complaint?

Approximately half my staff started as volunteers, and half my board started on volunteer committees. Volunteering is the way for them to love you and for you to love them. There is nothing they won't do for you or the organization; their loyalty is paramount. Working as a volunteer is a way of courting. Before you recruit someone to your board, you can see if you really like each other enough to get hitched. Because staff recruit volunteers, this gives you a way to recruit potential board members as volunteers first and groom them for board membership.

Planting Seeds

Getting to a point where you have an effective board
and volunteer corps is a long process. You must wade
into the politics, strengthen the board leadership, and
arm them with the information they need to achieve
the mission statement. This can take many years. But
the seeds you plant in your first hundred days—a review
of the bylaws, a commitment to improve the board,
and a retreat to set up a strategic plan and vision for the
future—will set the foundation for a strong future.

Review

- Executive directors do not control the board but
  must help lead them.
- An effective board has an even divide of the Three
  Ts: time, talent, and treasure.
- An effective board realizes that they are a "board of
  trustees," not a corporate "board of directors."
- An effective board has a plan in place to build the
  organization by imposing term limits and succession
  planning.
- An effective board is responsible for:

  e. Oversight of the executive director
  f. Succession planning and recruitment
  g. Fundraising, endowment, and development
  h. Strategic planning and vision (with the executive
     director)

    i. Oversight of accounting practices and accounts

    j. Infrastructure.

- An effective board understands they have responsibilities to invest in the organization, but that doesn't necessarily mean financially.
- An effective board contributes to an endowment.
- An effective board manages its time well.
- An effective board values all skills and actively recruits from the volunteer corps.
- Executive directors must plant the seeds to achieve an effective board and be patient.

Now that you have established a culture that is centered on the mission with a great attitude, a mission statement, a needs assessment, and an effective board, you are ready for a stakeholders' retreat to develop the vision of your organization. We do this through the strategic plan. This will not be a dusty document to be put in a drawer afterward. This strategic plan sets the tone for the future and develops ownership and change for years to come. Once your vision is established, dreams can come true.

Developing the Vision:
Strategic Planning with Stakeholders

Chapter 5

Without planning, no one ever heard of the explorer Don Gazpacho again.

It is a terrible thing to see and have no vision.
—Helen Keller

S o what does it mean to have "vision"? The diction-
ary has nine different definitions of vision. Helen
Keller's definition, and the one we are using, is "the
act or power of anticipating what will or may come to
be." This definition comes the closest but isn't ideal to
how we are defining vision. This isn't soothsaying. One
anticipates the future by planning. The idea of creating
vision in an organization is half based on fact and half
based on dreams, but it really must be equal parts of
both. The art of "vision making" is planning in such a
way that your dreams meet the facts halfway when you
see opportunities others may miss, and a path to those
dreams arises out of the fog.

You see opportunities where others see obstacles.
You see opportunities where others see nothing at all.
You see opportunities in every person you meet, every

non-profit you encounter, every business with which you work, and every patron who talks to you. Even when being criticized, you see it as an opportunity.

Once someone complained to me that my reports where badly written and my facts were not correct. Rather than argue with him, I just said, "You are right in that I am a terrible writer, and most of the people working with me are volunteers. We could use someone like you to help us edit the next report. Are you volunteering?"

When the city cut funding of our center, it was an opportunity to get press and start a membership drive. Every non-profit is a chance to partner strategically; I just have to figure out how. Our bank, our printer, our accountant—all offer opportunities to find sponsors, investors, board members, and patrons. This is vision. Where others see just a chance encounter, you see opportunities. It's the strategic planning process that will bring the collective vision to a material presence.

Let's get up to date and see where we are. I am counting your hundred days as business days, meaning five days a week. You have spent your first thirty to forty days (six to eight weeks):

- Assessing your organization and becoming an expert on it
- Interviewing staff and finding a consensus on possible problems
- Developing your team
- Having your staff work on a needs assessment
- Meeting with your inner circle of key stakeholders to

describe and get consensus on your early findings
Developing your board's expectations of themselves
- Setting up a key stakeholders' retreat

Preparing the Retreat

Somewhere around day thirty or forty, you will show up at an all-day (preferably) or half-day retreat. Your board president may have decided to have everyone out at his or her house to get away from everything. Maybe you are in a neutral park space. It's generally good to be far from normal office work, away from phones, and in a neutral environment. It could be at a park or under a tree.

Food is incredibly important for meetings, especially this one. Early in my career, I never wanted to have food at meetings because I was worried about the costs and the use of organizational funds to feed our stakeholders instead of spending it on the mission. But I discovered people bond over food. Nourishment of the body leads to nourishment of the spirit and brain. Religions are formed around meals. Nothing is more powerful for getting things done than breaking bread together. This is why we have state dinners with countries we don't like. When you are eating, you are more open and less cranky. It's essential to forwarding the mission. But don't wine and dine your people with expensive fare at the drop of a hat. Good food can be donated, cooked by volunteers, or bought at a reasonable price. Food at a meeting should be light and fun, not heavy, or people will fall asleep in the meeting.

After a long conference, retreat, or meeting such as

this is over, it's important to enjoy a bit of a party, which could mean serving moderate alcohol, or if the group is a cultural group, ethnic delicacies from that culture. If you decide to serve alcohol, it's important that the non-profit never pay for it. It must be donated. You don't want rumors to go out that organizational funds are being used to get the board drunk at meetings. Remember, things can get exaggerated. If your group is one that likes to drink, you will have no trouble finding someone willing to bring the booze. But remember, this is for AFTER the meeting is done.

The Facilitator

It's usually wise to bring in or hire a facilitator who has done strategic planning. This is important for a variety of reasons. Primarily this person is an outsider and will be treated with more respect than an insider, keeping things civil and focused. An outsider can also be stronger about facilitating so that one person doesn't dominate the conversation. It's possible that you, as a new director, might still get this kind of respect and can be an "outsider" enough to facilitate this. However, it's usually a smart move to get a total outsider. A director of a neighboring organization in another town might work. If you can't afford to pay a facilitator, maybe you can work out a trade: he or she facilitates your group, and you will do the same for him or her. Make sure you meet with your facilitator prior to the retreat and you are both on the same page as to what is expected. It wouldn't hurt if the facilitator reads this book so you both have the same frame of reference.

You will want to have giant presentation paper and markers so your facilitator can throw all the ideas up on the wall. A PowerPoint projector and laptop will also do the trick.

Icebreaker
The first order of business should be a 10- to 20-minute icebreaker—something that will put people at ease. It's good if it can make them feel a little stupid, too. Nothing bonds people more than having to drop their guard in front of one another. Icebreakers usually involve getting people to divulge something personal about themselves, so the walls are down and they are feeling as though they are among friends. You can use Google to find thousands of pages of icebreakers. Have fun picking one or give it to a key staff person to do. This gets them involved— preferably someone who is very social. It might be, "You are on a desert island stranded for a very long time. What three things would you bring and why?"

Now we are ready to begin. Here are the things that should be in your strategic plan:

1. Needs Assessment and Mission Statement
Now that people are relaxed and bonding, you can give them the results of the needs assessment so they

can feel the importance of your mission. Make sure you compliment those who did the research and put it together for you. Whoever said "Flattery gets you nowhere" was an idiot. True and honest compliments are the best way to bond with people. Beginning with the needs assessment drives home the point that everything centers on the mission.

The next thing to do is to get agreement on the mission statement. If you have not done this previously, expect that it can take as long as two hours to debate. Getting the right verbiage is important. Since everything else rests on this, it shouldn't be rushed. Stakeholders must feel this is their mission, not yours. Nothing can come of vision until the mission statement is well defined and agreed upon by all stakeholders.

The facilitator might start by writing the current mission statement on the paper large enough so all can see. Then he or she would say, "After hearing the needs assessment, do we all agree that this states our mission in the best way, succinctly and with measurable objectives?" That will turn into a major discussion in most places. Some will say it's too vague, while others think vague is good. The facilitator must keep the discussion moving forward by:

- Not letting people rehash what has already been agreed upon
- Not letting things get off topic on tangents with "Save that discussion for when we get to that subject"
- Not letting people make personal attacks—this is about the mission, not old arguments

- Picking apart elements to focus on when things get too wild or vague—"Let's just focus on the measurable objectives; can we measure this?"
- Blaming no one but the facilitator when things go awry

Facilitators absorb blame, keeping everyone else free to be productive and bond. Remember what we learned in leadership: facilitators don't have any answers; they are just the ones holding the flashlight in the dark tunnel. And the facilitator doesn't have to work with these people the next day. So it's OK if he or she gets a bit bloody. Facilitators fall on the grenade to save the team.

1. Not Voting on Things. Voting Is a System Of Democracy, Not Consensus.

Reaching consensus isn't about doing what the majority like. Consensus is about getting all those at the table to agree to a set of ideas. They don't all have to love the ideas. But they all have to agree to them and be comfortable enough with them to feel good about implementing them and owning them.

A great tool for this approach that I learned while a Coro Fellow is a technique called "Fist to Five." In this technique you ask people to show how much they like the idea presented by putting up fingers on their right hand. Those who love the idea put up five fingers. Those who don't put up one finger (not the middle one!). This means they are not crazy about it but can live with it. They can put up any number of fingers in between to

describe their feelings on the subject. The facilitator can
tell the reaction to an idea by counting the fingers or
just seeing its popularity, like a poll. However, stakeholders who hate the idea can put up a fist. If they do, the
idea is blocked and can't move forward; however, the
person putting up the fist has to address all present explaining why he or she hates the idea. In the discussion
things may change. The objection may be addressed, or
the person who put up the fist may prevail in convinc-
ing others it's not a good idea at this time. In this way
the facilitator can get a better idea of the consensus
than a simple majority vote would do. If one person
puts up a fist, this is a good indication he or she would
work to undermine the project if it had been voted on
with a simple majority. Therefore, it's more productive
to address this when the idea is presented than down
the road when there is a great deal invested in the idea.

Facilitators are like sheep dogs herding the flock by
heading them off at the pass when they want to run
on tangents or when they panic. Facilitators are calm,
supportive, and loving of all. Consensus building has to
be a very loving process built on respect.

2. SWOT Analysis

Once the mission statement is addressed and agreed to,
the facilitator would ask the following question: "What
makes us unique?" This is important, as the answers you
get will help define your unique place in the community,
which can lead to fundraising and help the mission. This

could be "We are the only provider of low-cost health-care in the region" or "we give shoes to people who can't afford them—no one else is doing that in the state."

The facilitator will follow this up with the SWOT analysis, which concentrates the discussion on strengths, weaknesses, opportunities, and threats.

Strengths. "What are our strengths?" Your strengths could be things like a strong board, a long and great reputation, great staff, a new building, or equipment. If someone says great new leadership, either you have made a good first impression or a staff member is brown-nosing. (Probably a bit of both, but either way it's nice to hear.)

Weaknesses. "What are our weaknesses?" Weaknesses could be problems that have come up. The last direc-tor alienated a group of supporters. A portion of the community perceives you as enabling gang members instead of getting people out of gangs because of a mis-perception of a past incident. A civic leader isn't a fan of your group and works against you in public, in private, or both. I have actually seen all of these come up in past experience.

Opportunities. "What opportunities exist?" These usu-ally are ways to address the weaknesses. We can work as a team to bring back the alienated supporters into the fold and make that a priority. We can produce a new marketing campaign to explain our program with gangs better and use the controversy to get press and get our message out. We can partner with the civic leader's favorite non-profit on a program that might get the leader involved with us in a positive way.

Threats. "What are our threats?" Threats are usually problems we don't yet have but are likely to happen. These could be: The economy gets worse and hurts fundraising, our federal grant that pays 50 percent of our budget dries up, or a key staff person who does 80 percent of the work leaves or retires. These present new opportunities to go back later and diversify fundraising or staffing or develop a succession plan, and so on. Noticing threats is part of vision thinking. Visionaries are people who can see problems before they happen and find opportunities before they become evident.

Once the SWOT analysis is done, it would be a good time for a break. Let people have fifteen minutes (no more or you will never get them back) to use the restroom, check their messages, discuss what has happened, and finish a snack.

3. Goals

Now comes goal setting. During the break, the facilitator has put on the wall three large pieces of paper, each blank except for one question at the top. The first says, "What is our chief program (or staff) goal?" If your organization has multiple programs or sites, there may be one of these for each. One says, "What is our chief board goal?" and the final one says, "What is our chief financial goal?"

The facilitator will tell everyone to close their eyes and pretend it's three years into the future. Then our facilitator will have the stakeholders put up ideas as bullet points on the program goal sheet. Remember these are goals for three years hence. You must be realistic as to what could happen in three years without being too conservative. A lot can happen in three years. People tend to underestimate their capabilities.

They can be debated, merged, and rescinded, but in the end the group must come to agreement on which goal is the highest priority. It's important to understand at this point the difference between the goal and an objective. Goals are the end zone to which you hope to carry the ball for a touchdown. In the corporate world, they are sometimes called BHAGs—Big Hairy Audacious (or Achievable) Goals, meaning a goal that is really a dream you can only do with great effort, but is doable. BHAGs are what you are looking for— goals that challenge the organization to live up to the mission in a big way.

An objective is a smaller "first down" needed to get to the end zone. For example, if the goal is to serve a free after-school nutrition program to all two hundred kids who live in your service area and you are now serving twelve kids, an objective might be to create more space to serve food in or to get donations of more food. These are things needed to get to the big GOAL. The facilitator might see that some of the "goals" written on the paper are actually objectives for a bigger goal and incorporate them. In the end each question should have ONE goal answer with objectives to reach that one goal.

This is what the entire stakeholders' retreat has been about. It all comes down to this point. It's important to get them all on the same page: thinking about the mission; identifying problems and fixes; re-energizing them for the road ahead. But this is the exercise that will really make them work for the mission. Because the bullet points that end up on these giant sheets of presentation paper are not just words on a page. These goals are not YOUR goals. These ideas are not YOUR ideas. These goals are THEIR goals and THEIR ideas that came from THEIR mouths and floated across the room onto the paper with THEIR agreement. When they leave this retreat, they are not going to be handed a document with what you as a leader want them to do as followers, which will ultimately sit in a drawer for three years and do nothing except allow you to say to funders you did a strategic plan. When you leave the retreat, they will receive a document with a few clear, concise goals on it that THEY came up with and clear objectives to reach those goals. Now they are invested because they are investing in their own idea. It's much easier to get people to work hard and put up money when they have stock in the company. People have much more energy to implement their own ideas then yours. You have given them ownership of the mission and goals and sent them off with their own flashlights, to their own dark tunnels to lead their own groups forward for the mission. This is incredibly empowering. They OWN the mission now. And they know what the goal is because it's their own goal.

From a leadership standpoint, your staff and stakeholders will be harder to control than in a conventional system with a boss and employees. It will be a little like herding cats. Now that they OWN the mission and the goals, they no longer work for you. They now work for the mission. All you can do if they get lost is remind them of that fact. People who work for a mission are harder to control, but it's much easier for them to be successful. They will work many more hours without supervision and get things done because they care about the mission. They will also argue with you about the interpretation of the mission. But because you are bonded by the mission, it will be done with respect.

Once the group has decided on the primary goal for programs (meaning also for staff since staff carry out programs), they can decide on the basic steps to reach that BHAG. In order to serve more kids, we need more volunteers. How do we recruit them? We need more space. Where can we partner to get space after school? We need more donations of food. With whom can we partner to get more food?

Notice I never said anything about money. It's my belief you can get more money for your mission by not talking about money. As a non-profit you must talk about your budget, but you don't have to be someone always asking for money. If a homeless man has a sign that says "Will work for food" and another has a sign that says "Give me $20," which are you more willing to help? But you are not likely to give the man with the "Work for Food" sign a sandwich or even a job. You are more likely to give him money because it's fast and easy for you and makes you feel good that you helped. The same is true of non-profits. If we focus on what we need—volunteers, food, and space for an after-school nutrition program—someone might give us space or someone might give us money to rent space. Someone might give us food or money to buy food. But if we just asked for money to fund the whole program at a large price tag, it would seem like an insurmountable price, and we would get nothing.

This strategy is called zero budgeting. You concentrate on the task and the needs irrespective of costs, looking first for in-kind donations (meaning donations of actual items, not money), and then money only when the items can't be secured. Faith-based organizations have made an art form of this approach. The reverend will preach on Sunday how the church needs a new roof, and if only God will provide! And after the sermon a parishioner will come up and say, "I'm a contractor, Father. I will build you a roof," or say, "My company will pay for the roof, Reverend, if you put a plaque up to acknowledge the donation and give me the write-off."

Once I ran a cultural center out of an old firehouse near the docks in the harbor area of LA. I was told it was to serve as an arts center while a new arts center was being built nearby. I also had no budget to do anything but hire teachers for programs. I met with over a dozen non-profits in the community over the next six months.

An oil refinery offered to renovate the space for free as a team-building project. They painted and built the stages, recording studio, computer lab, and dance studio in two weeks, with most of the work happening on one Friday "build day." A local ballet company donated the flooring materials and air conditioners with the agreement they would teach classes in the space. A non-profit gang-prevention program donated a copy machine when they upgraded. A local foundation paid for the equipment to build a recording studio in the space. A computer-recycling firm gave us twenty used computers for a computer lab. All totaled, over $200,000 in goods and services were donated without a penny changing hands. The center went from serving twelve kids a week to serving over 540 kids a week in less than a year. This is what can be done with zero budgeting.

Once the BHAG for a program is done, you will do the same for the board. "Where do you see the board in three years in a perfect world? What is your dream board that can be achieved?" This could be to recruit some needed new members with skills the board needs, such as a lawyer, accountant, printer, or web guru. It could be for the board to set a new fundraising goal. It could be to rewrite the bylaws, which are woefully out of date. These could all be objectives to a goal of doubling your board or cutting down your board to a more reasonable size. But whatever you decide, it should come primarily from the board members at the meeting.

Once this is all done, you might want to take another break. During the break, you as the executive director, along with the bookkeeper, the facilitator, and the board president, should have a little huddle. You might look at the goals that have been decided and try to estimate a price tag of what it might cost to implement these goals. Even if the goals are accomplished by in-kind donation of goods and services rather than actual money changing hands, it still counts the same as if someone wrote you a check for the full amount, such as in the example of my firehouse. That added $200,000 to my income budget just as if a check had paid for it all. But it also added $200,000 to my expenses. In-kind donations are always recorded in both the income and expense lines.

Once you have an idea of what the costs of your goals might be, you can reconvene everyone in the room. The facilitator will show them the price tags you have come up with for the goals you have set. You can discuss whether the group agrees with your assessment. Make sure you build in 10–15 percent for administration costs over the program costs. Once there is consensus on the price of the program goal and the board goal, you can set the final goal for the organization, which is a goal for your budget in three years when these goals are reached. The price for these goals might be $250,000, and you might have to increase your current budget of $500,000 by 50 percent to accomplish the goals. Therefore your financial goal will be "To increase our budget by 50 percent in three years."

You might state some objectives of how to get there with donated space, food, and volunteers, but also with new grants for the new initiative, or new funding from the community. We will discuss this in depth when we get to fundraising. An objective might be simply to identify community partners, identify sources of income and grants, recruit more volunteers, or recruit back alumni of the program.

Once this piece is done, it's party time! Let the stakeholders bond over wine and cheese, a home-cooked potluck meal, or donated catering. Let them eat, drink, and be merry, for a new day has dawned. But you must know your work isn't done here. This is only the beginning of a process for you. You can revel momentarily in your accomplishments. You've reenergized your base. You've led them to consensus. You have given them a new start, a rebirth, and you can feel the energy in the room.

4. Budget

The real work begins after the retreat. You sit with your accountant and create a spreadsheet that looks like the table on the following page.

You might have detailed rows of income such as earned income and donated income; and expenses such as programs, fundraising, marketing, and administration. You should have last fiscal year's numbers ready to go and a good projection on what is happening this year. You can then fill in the numbers for Plan Year 3, which is what your goal numbers should be. It isn't hard to look at your goals and guess how much of the increased budget might come from earned income versus donated income, or how much will be program expenses versus

	Last Fiscal Year	Current Fiscal Year	Plan Year 1	Plan Year 2	Plan Year 3
Income					
Expense					

Figure 1. *Example budget table.*

administration. (Tip: Administration would never be more than one-third and should be closer to 15 to 25 percent of your budget and never less than 10 percent. Do not put salaries of program personnel in administration. If executive staff do some program work, figure out a formula of what percentage is program and put that in program expenses.)

Once you have the Plan Year 3 goals and objectives written out from the big sheets onto a document and the budget spelled out, you can do a backward timeline. This is where you figure out Plan Year 2 goals and Plan Year 1 goals based on where you are and where you want to be. For example, let's go back to our after-school nutrition program. You currently serve twelve kids after school and want to serve two hundred kids in three years. In two years you want to get to a hundred, meaning that next year you must get to fifty. So you identify ways to increase to fifty, with a plan to double each year after. Where are you going to get the space, help, and food? You have identified a non-profit pantry that will donate the food if you serve more kids, so that is taken care of. You identify a park space nearby that will accommodate your program in the first year until you can find a bigger space. So all you must do is put the call out for more volunteers. You figure out the in-kind donated cost of food and rental of space and put it in the budget. You will have to pay for marketing to get the volunteers and participants. You put that figure in the budget. You will need to find donations for the marketing. You know that a new Boys & Girls Club is being built on your block, and they could partner with a bigger space in year two and may even help pay for costs. Now your plan is really coming together.

By the end of two weeks after the retreat (around day forty, or eight weeks), you will have a finished strategic plan report to present to the board. It will include these eleven items:

1. A cover page with a pretty picture that speaks to your mission
2. Your newly agreed-upon mission statement
3. A paragraph about the process you used to get the plan, acknowledging the facilitator, staff who did the needs assessment, and stakeholders who organized the retreat
4. Your needs assessment
5. Your business concept (what makes you unique)
6. A history of your organization
7. A list of staff and board with short biographies and maybe pictures of key people
8. Your SWOT analysis
9. Your three-year goals and objectives
10. A budget showing how you are going to get there
11. A concluding paragraph to rally the troops

Item 3 will help you document for posterity what

happened. The mission statement and items 4–7 are all things you will need for grant proposals. Now that you have this plan, you can just cut and paste this info into grant documents, saving your staff lots of time and making documents consistent. Items 9 and 10 will need to be updated quarterly or annually, depending on your process. You will make a PDF of the document and print enough copies for the stakeholders, members, alumni, grants, and strategic partnerships. You may need fifty to three hundred copies. Put one copy in your archives for documentation.

You are now forty to fifty days into the process (ten weeks). By this point your board and staff are incredibly impressed with your leadership. The way you rallied the troops, focused the mission, and created the plan was incredible. Now everyone is on the same page with clear and concise goals that will turn your dreams into reality, a map to get there, and a focus on mission. At the next board meeting, they vote to pass the strategic plan.

Another Way

When I started at the Muck, I had been doing strategic plans the way I describe for over a decade with great success. But I quickly realized the Muck was different and would require a different approach. The Muck was over forty years old as an organization when I arrived and was deeply entrenched in the community, with four distinct communities of stakeholders involved in visual arts, arts education, performing arts, and historic elements. There were two separate support groups—a men's group for the car show fundraiser and a women's group that ran our gift shop; as well as the board, and several groups of stakeholders trying to become involved in the Muck but not completely accepted by those in charge.

I decided a single stakeholders group would not serve the mission. Therefore, during my first hundred days, I set up ten different "focus groups" of stakeholders with ten separate meetings doing the strategic planning process. These groups were:

1. Staff
2. Seniors (our support groups)
3. Youth outreach
4. Korean outreach[1]
5. Latino outreach
6. Visual arts community
7. Performing arts community
8. Arts education community
9. Business leaders and board
10. Non-profit leaders

Each group came up with a goal that was synthesized into a goal for each of the four program areas. From these meetings also came a clear picture of what we needed

---

1   *Koreans and Latinos make up the two largest non-White groups in town (as of this printing).*

to do with our capital campaign. This was a longer, more difficult process, but it went miles toward reconnecting stakeholders who had long since dropped off to the organization and mission. It also brought in some new people.

When we conducted a new plan three years later, we went back to a single stakeholder retreat because the organization was cohesive and successful by then.

Vision Thinking

Creating a strategic plan is very important to success, but you can't just think about the future once every three years. You must think years down the road all the time. When you meet with strategic partners, think about what the future might hold for these partnerships. When you hear about changes in government, politics, businesses, other non-profits, the community, or any major change in town, you should ask yourself how this will affect your organization in the future. Will it have repercussions for you? Are there opportunities for you?

Don't make your decisions based solely on what effect a crisis or opportunity has on you today, but what the future might hold. For example, we planned a capital campaign at the Muck for 2015. We started planning it back in 2007. Originally it was set for 2008, but the plan was not widely liked by the community when I came on board. We decided to wait till 2015 because that allowed us not to compete with other capital campaigns in the area. We would have time to get their support, and it gave us a longer timeline to raise funds. We could also revamp our plans by consensus. In addition, 2015 is our fiftieth anniversary, giving us another marketing tool for the campaign. In 2009, when the economy was bad, we were glad we postponed. But there were some in our group of stakeholders who thought we should scrap the plans altogether, saying this was a terrible time to talk about building something when the city was cutting budgets and things were so grim. If I thought in the present, I would have agreed. But instead we forged ahead. We spent the last three years gathering support, receiving a grant to conduct the master plan, and getting our house in order. Now we are on target for our capital project with a new strategic plan and funding commitments in place.

I could write an entire book on the craft of strategic and visionary thinking. It's simply a process of having a sense of climate. It's not much different from predicting the weather. You see what is coming and make conservative guesses as to what the climate brings. Things such as the economy, budget cuts, school closings, financial windfalls, new laws, and major news stories all have a major effect on communities, and therefore on you. Everything is an opportunity. If a school closes, does that present an opportunity for you to do more work in the affected neighborhood? If a new tax provides a windfall, is there a way your mission is eligible for some of the funds? If a young girl is murdered in your community, spawning a new movement, does your mission become part of that movement? Everything that happens becomes related to your mission. It's like Sudoku. You can't add a number to the board without its affecting every other number on the board. Your community is a Sudoku board in that respect. You must grow and change with every other change, but try to always stay two steps ahead.

Constant reassessment of planning and vision is the difference between an organization that is constantly growing and one that is stagnant. The faster you grow, the more you must reassess. Once you get close to meeting your goals, it's time to make new ones. If you don't, your growth will stop. If you haven't drawn an end zone, where does your team run for a touchdown?

Don't be afraid to experiment. Successful organizations do not happen overnight. They happen by study, evaluation, planning, execution, and making mistakes; and then by studying the mistakes, evaluation, planning, execution, and making fewer mistakes. The cycle keeps going until you achieve success. Then people will say you got there overnight and effortlessly. But you will know the truth.

Review

1. Remember that strategic planning sets the vision for the organization if it's a consensus process created for a stakeholders' retreat.
2. Create a neutral space for the retreat with food and a nurturing atmosphere.

3. Bring in or hire a neutral facilitator who has done strategic planning.

4. Make the first order of business some sort of ice-breaker to put people at ease.

5. Review the needs assessment with the group, then agree on the mission statement by consensus.

6. Conduct a SWOT analysis. (Strengths, Weaknesses, Opportunities, Threats)

7. Decide on a Big Hairy Achievable Goal for staff or program and one for the board, and a financial goal for three years in the future by consensus.

8. After the retreat create a backward timeline and budget for your goals.

9. Write and review your strategic plan with the board. After approval it can be published. Put it every-where—post it on your website, send it to your investors and stakeholders, and publish it in the community. Be proud you have a plan.

10. Continue thinking strategically about the future in all aspects of your work.

Now that you have a plan and everyone is on board following you to achieve your organizational dreams, you are going to need to expand your leadership to the community at large and form strategic partnerships within the community to accomplish your goals. It's time to put together a resource map to help you forge ahead.

Networks:
Resource Mapping The Community

Chapter 6

If you have come to help me, you are wasting your time.
But if you have come because your liberation is bound up
with mine, then let's work together.

—Aboriginal Activists Group from Queensland, NZ

The word "community" comes from the Latin word for "common place." In most ancient societies, land, water, and other resources were not owned by a few but were shared by all. The tribe shared everything outside your personal home. And the tribe worked together to take care of the sick and elderly, raise the children, and feed the village. With modern capitalism we changed to the concept of ownership of shared resources and a few owning that which is used by the many.

It's in sharing resources and clients that non-profits differ from both faith-based organizations and corporations. Ironically, non-profits generally do a better job of sharing resources than our faith-based counterparts do with one another. This isn't because of competition,

but because faith-based organizations often see themselves as too different from other faith-based groups
to share. When I was running prison arts programs,
we lent our guitars to the Muslim chaplain because
the Christian chaplain refused to allow the "Muslim
heathens" to play their guitars. This is an extreme incident and not very Christian. However, it drives home
the point that faith-based organizations have a hard
enough time talking to one another, let alone sharing
resources. More wars have been fought over faith than
any other reason.

Corporations don't share resources well because
of a fear of helping the competition. But in the non-
profit world, we have no competition. Anyone who
says otherwise is wrong. Every non-profit has a unique
mission. If two have the same mission, then there is
no need for the second one. Even if there are several
non-profit theatres in town, they each serve a different
purpose. One may do large musical theatre produc-
tions, another opera, a third Shakespeare, a fourth
improvisational theatre, and a fifth new works by
local artists and writers. If every mission is unique in a
community, then they have little to lose by sharing resources and everything to gain. Is it possible you might
lose an investor to another organization with whom
you partner? It's possible. But it's more likely you will
get several investors from the partnership you never
had before. Most people who invest in community
non-profits invest in several things that are important
to them, not just one charity.

Strategic Partnerships

The only way a community gets stronger is when resources are shared. This is the only way non-profits get stronger. The cornerstone of success as a non-profit director is from strategic partnerships.

What is a strategic partnership? It's a combined and committed effort in which both partners receive something or are improved somehow. As a director of arts programs, I have partnered with other arts programs to create cooperative marketing plans and festivals that help all our non-profits get more patrons. A musical theatre that serves mostly seniors tries to get the younger demographic. It partners with a ninety-nine-seat experimental theatre that is trying to get the older, more monied patrons. They both gain by cross marketing. If each puts an ad in the other's programs with a coupon at no cost, the ninety-nine-seat theatre may get some older patrons coming in and maybe some new investors, while the musical theatre may get some younger patrons who will help sustain it into the future.

I have partnered with social service groups like foster care and shelters to provide arts programs to their clients. This helps me have a strong program for a grant and helps them better serve their clients. A study showed that their non-English-speaking clients learned English more quickly when our art programs ran in their site. This helped them get a federal grant for the program, which gave us a contract tripling our programs.

I have partnered with a senior center to provide free classes in our arts center. They pay the teacher and we provide the space, and we both serve more people in our missions. Many of their students are now members and patrons of our other paying programs.

We rent our beautiful historic building when we are not using it for extra income. We host approximately seventy-five weddings each year, which pays 30 percent of our bills. We started making the site available to other non-profits for fundraising events at a reduced rental because they can rent on weeknights we are normally closed. We get more rental fees, and they get a low-cost site to use.

These examples are just the tip of the iceberg. Each year my non-profit partners with sixty-five to eighty different community non-profit partners. We also partner with approximately twenty for-profit and government businesses. Grants and funding are a kind of strategic partnership in which they invest in your mission and you fulfill their mission of making the community stronger.

I will warn you: if you are ardent in finding community partnerships, you will have some that fail and fail miserably. There will be deadbeat partners who promise the world and do not deliver. There will be group consortia that start out with everyone singing "Kumbaya" and holding hands, and end up with you doing all the work to see it to fruition. They might even be happy to take the credit for all your work. These nightmare partnerships happen. But they are the minority. And when partnerships work, the partners become great resources for you to rely on. Both your organizations flourish. It's worth the few bad experiences for the many good ones.

Resource Mapping

No one is so plugged in to our communities that we just know who all the strategic partnering possibilities are. We all think we are THAT plugged in. But in reality, the possibilities are limitless. Every time you turn over a new rock, you will be astounded by what you find. This is where resource mapping comes in.

Resource mapping is simply listing and mapping the resources that exist in your community. It must be updated every year because they constantly evolve. New directors and staff come and go. Locations change. This process is long and tedious, but it will help you in many ways you never even suspected. The initial work can be done by a staff member or team with interns and volunteers. It could be the same people who did the needs assessment since it's similar research work. In large cities now, there are websites that have done this work for you and created resource maps, but they are never complete because they only get data from limited sources. A good resource map will list the following:

- Community public and private schools
- After-school programs and youth services
- Faith-based programs
- Senior programs and services
- Early childhood services for 0–5 years old

- Colleges and universities
- Hospitals and health care networks
- Shelters for homeless people, battered women, human trafficking victims, drug rehabilitation patients, and so on
- Prison ministries and halfway houses
- Gang prevention programs
- Hotlines for rape, suicide prevention, and so on
- City, county, and other government run programs and grants
- Recreational facilities
- Arts and cultural organizations
- Museums, historical groups, and heritage sites
- Legal aid services
- Food banks
- Foundations and grant makers

Each site or service should be listed on a spreadsheet in Microsoft Excel like in the table.

By using Excel, you can organize it by rows or columns for viewing. You can then import it into Google Drive for free and share it with others at your organization. You can tell the marketing director to talk to like organizations about working together on marketing. You can tell your program director to look for strategic partners on programs that fit with the new strategic plan goals. You can email newsletters to all or some on your resource map and invite them to an event you are doing or give them a non-profit discount on membership or merchandise. You can email them to help peti-

	Contact 1	...
Agency	Boys & Girls Club of Timbuktu	
Type	Youth Services	
Contact	John Doe	
Position	Executive Director	
Phone	(555) 555-1212	
Email	Jdoe@bgct.org	
Address	555 W 5th St. 90001	

Figure 1. Resource Map detail. In the full table, you'll want column headers for agency, type, contact, position, phone, email, and address.

tion elected officials or vote on legislation that affects your organization (and maybe theirs). Now you have created a lobby, making you a political leader in your city. But you must be careful about this. There are laws against non-profits taking political stands for or against an elected official or party, but you can let people know about an issue that affects you without taking a partisan stand.

You can add the finished resource map to your strategic plan. You can make it into a resource guide to give to your clients so they can find other services in the area that will help them. You can add numbered dots to a street map of your community corresponding to numbers on your resource list at their addresses. This will tell you which agencies serve your direct neighborhood. It will also tell you where there is no coverage and where there may be a need for some help. How impressed will stakeholders be when you tell them you are expanding to Pumpernickel Street because they are completely without services, as you discovered with

your resource map? How great would that be for potential clients on Pumpernickel Street who have never
had any help while people wonder why the crime rate
is so high there?

Each of us helps the community in different ways,
and by integrating our services, we can help the
community the most. There are people out there who
will resent this approach and may even hate you for it.
I have my share of detractors because of this. Generally these people do very little for the community and
are comfortable. They want to go on doing very little
and feel as if they are doing something great. You use
the same advice with people like this that your mom
gave you for bullies at school—ignore them. Not
everyone will like you, especially if you are making
changes. Some people hate change. You can't worry
about them.

When I did my first resource map many years ago,
it was a twelve-block radius of the harbor area of Los
Angeles, and we identified 105 agencies that worked
in that twelve square blocks. We couldn't believe how
many there were. We had expected we might find
thirty agencies. Those were 105 potential partners for
anything we needed—space to do programs, clients
to serve, volunteers to help, staff to recruit, partners
to work with on funding, grants, or programs. If each
agency had an average of a dozen people working at
them as staff, board members, and volunteers, that was
a network of 1,260 people. Most non-profit people are
avid voters, and in most towns, elections are won by

fewer than a thousand votes. Therefore you have the potential to create a lobby of voters that can sway an election (not that you would use the power to endorse candidates, which non-profits can't do). As a small non-profit, you would not have enough sway to get the attention of politicians who can help you in your cause, but as a lobby of more than 1,200 people, you can get almost anything done. What happens when 1,200 people work together?

This map of the Harbor City community of Los Angeles led to my organizing a youth conference and inviting all 105 potential partners. It was an all-day conference with break-out sessions on different issues pertaining to youth. That summit led to a resource guide, a referral service, and many partnerships. Everything gets better when colleagues talk.

Currently, I belong to five e-village networks and two non-profit collaborative agencies that do nothing but partnering between non-profits. Through these groups we discuss problems that arise, find training, mentor others, lobby legislation, get mentored by others, send out staff recruitments, find volunteers, market to one another or cooperatively to the public, and even share funding sources. I have one partner who sends me lots of grant information knowing that I will find a grant now and then on which we can partner. One e-village compares notes on new regulations, going rates for artist fees, and whether or not an artist is good to work with. Another e-village sends out job announcements, new classes starting, and grant information.

Networks

Once you have a list of all the services available in your community, try to network with them. Many communities have some sort of collaborative of local non-profits. If yours has one, become active in it. I hear non-profit leaders say, "I don't have time for outside activities. I have to focus on my non-profit." But they don't realize how much more successful they would be by networking. As an executive director, I spend approximately 25 percent of my time networking. That is one of the keys to my success. That networking has led to a doubling of budget and tripling of programs or more in almost every post I have held.

Networking also provides job security in an insecure non-profit world. With networks you are the first to hear of job openings and more likely to know the movers and shakers in these organizations should you want to change positions. A well-networked successful leader will never be out of work for long.

Whether or not your area has such a network, reserve a day once a week or several hours each day to go out and meet others in the community. Have board members introduce you to other non-profit directors with whom they work on other boards. Call other directors on the resource map and say, "I see we serve the same clients. Would you like to have lunch sometime and see how we can work better together?" I have rarely had a lunch like this without something great happening from it. At the Muck I had lunch with the director of a local foster care agency. It led to a $70,000-a-year contract to conduct arts classes with her sites. I find networking lunches to be most effective. I have one almost every day. It becomes another great perk of my job that I get a lunch on partners or my organization every day, but I make those lunches back manyfold in new investment.

Other Networks

Networks will go beyond non-profits and include service clubs and chambers of commerce. Networking is key to your job. After all, the major difference between a director of operations and a CEO or executive director is that the COO is concerned with the day-to-day running of the organization. A CEO is concerned with the vision and future of an organization. In most small- and mid-sized non-profits, the CEO sometimes has to be the COO and development director too. In my job I wear all three hats. It's the networking that will distinguish you from being just a COO who is keeping the ship afloat. Without networking you are in the office treading water for the status quo. You will never get anywhere. If you need something and you cold call someone you barely know, will you get it? Maybe one time out of a hundred you will. But if you are out networking, you are calling a friend. Networking results in new strategic partnerships, new funding, and new patrons, growing your mission and meeting your goals. It's networking that makes you an explorer going where no man has gone before.

Networking really must start in the third week. Just
after you evaluate your organization and staff in the first
two weeks, you should be out attending community
breakfasts, lunches, fundraising dinners, and weekend
fundraisers for other groups. Your first hundred days
we count in business days, but you will not be working
business days. Tell your spouse he or she will not see you
for five months. Say good-bye to family and friends for
five months. Your first hundred days calculated at five
days a week will actually be seven days a week, twelve
hours a day, and seem more like 140 long days. It will be
exhausting. It will be exhilarating.

If you follow the advice in this book and work cheerfully, by the end of twenty weeks, you will be greeted as
the savior of the town. People will start talking about
running you for political office. You will have to find
ways of turning down all the invites you get for parties.
And, most important, people will start to invest in you,
your organization, and your mission.

Most people, hearing they will be expected to work
twelve-hour days, seven days a week for five months,
would prepare their resignation letter. But you are
different. This is different. Your marathon start to your
job isn't stressful. It's not really even work. This is part
of the attitude we talked about in Leadership. We have
amazing jobs where we get to do amazing work. If you
tell people you are working twelve hours a day seven
days a week, they will feel very bad for you. But if you
tell them your job is to attend lunches, breakfasts, golf
tournaments, card parties, performances, walking tours,

and multicourse dinners, they will not feel so bad. This IS your job, and you get paid to do it. Your job is to be a wonderful, happy person whom people want to be around. Your job is to talk about the great organization you represent and how it gets better every day.

Your organization will be paying for all the fees, lunches, dinners, and parties—not you. At the Muck we spend approximately $2,500 a year on dues, lunches, fundraisers, and fees for networking. We give away about a hundred auction items in memberships and tickets every year to other people's fundraisers, which costs us very little and brings people to us. But the payoff for this small investment is over $200,000 in new investment.

If you do your job of being an all-around fun guy or girl at functions as well as being a good leader in your organization, you have mastered the craft of being a great executive director for a non-profit. Remember the S=LMV formula. Leadership isn't just leading your organization in a dark tunnel but leading the community too, with a great attitude and a can-do spirit. If you do that while promoting the mission and vision (goals), you will be successful. Success = Leadership + Mission + Vision. This is most true in your networks.

So how do you get into the dozens of important networks that exist in your community? Most networks are looking for new members. They want you as much as you want them. Once you join them, you will find they become very important to you too. After you have joined the non-profit networks such as non-profit collaborative and professional e-villages, move on to other networks.

If you work with youth, join a youth collaborative network. If you work in health care, join a medical collaborative network. You can find them by asking colleagues, searching online, or by asking board members who have been around a while and serve on multiple boards. If you are under thirty-five, you might want to see if there are young professional networks in your area.

To find e-villages—groups that only exist online and have no formal meetings—ask colleagues or try Yahoo Groups. Most e-villages at the time of this writing are moderated through a listserve or through Yahoo Groups. Another service for groups is MeetUp.com. Electronic Virtual Community Networks (sometimes called e-villages) are great for asking technical questions of colleagues, posting announcements, or finding resources others use.

In our office currently, each of my staff belongs to multiple networks. Our marketing director belongs to a marketing roundtable of museum professionals. Our administrator belongs to an HR directors' roundtable and an insurance issues e-village put out by our non-profit insurance provider. Our curator is part of the National Association of Museums and a curator's e-village. Our education director is part of a countywide arts education roundtable that meets monthly and has an e-village. We all belong to the LA Culture Net (a Yahoo Group moderated by the Los Angeles County Arts Commission). I belong to the California Presenters, which has an e-village of people who present artists on stages across the state. We are part of the Association of Fundraising Professionals, which works to facilitate fundraising in the region. They are an international group. I am part of the Western Alliance of Arts Administrators, a regional group that presents artists in the Western United States. I am part of a Los Angeles-based collaborative I helped found called the Joint Agency Meeting, the Fullerton Collaborative of Educational Non-profits, the North Orange County Coordinating Council of Historical Agencies, the Los Angeles Heritage Group of LA Regional Historical Agencies, and more. Some of these groups host a monthly or quarterly meeting. Others are simply e-villages that are there when you have a question or an answer to others' questions, and they just come as emails. All are important in some way to our success. You can be involved with them as little or as much as you need. They are low maintenance.

Once you get to figuring out how to manage these groups, they become easy to control. You can direct staff to go to some of the meetings once your presence is established. Many of the emails you can screen from your inbox before even opening them. I get 150 emails each day but only need to read approximately a third of them.

Chambers of Commerce

When you establish yourself with the non-profit networks, make a point to attend some chamber of commerce events. A chamber of commerce is a network for the business community in your town. Some are stronger than others. Some events within the chamber are more well attended than others. However, a chamber can be a gateway to corporate sponsorship, new board members, strategic partners, and more. The strangest thing is that very few non-profits take advantage of chamber membership. Those that do join tend to reap many benefits because they are talking to business on their own terms.

At the Muck, I joined our local chamber in my first week. Two years later our organization had doubled its corporate sponsorship and received the chamber award for non-profit of the year. I was awarded Chamber Ambassador of the Year. These events were linked. It was my cultivation of the chamber relationships that led both to the recognition and the doubling of corporate sponsorships. Now, five years later, we belong to four chambers, and sponsorship continues to rise as our service area increases. We now serve eight outreach sites accounting for an 800 percent increase in our student population and $200,000 of our budget increase. Many of these contacts started at chamber events.

Faith-Based

If there are faith-based networks, join them. Faith-based organizations, as we discussed earlier, tend to be more insular and you may have to seek them out, but it can add a great new dimension to your organization. Let's say, for example, your area has a large Iranian population. Wouldn't you want to reach out to the Islamic centers and Mosques in your area and network with them? They may need your services and may have funding for your type of program, which they don't have the expertise to start on their own. Because they are insular, they have no idea you exist and are used to not interacting with the community at large outside their own, partially due to the anti-Muslim sentiments that have been whipped up by the media since 9/11. How do you think they will feel when you meet with them, offer partnership while eating lunch in an Iranian restaurant with them, and work out ways you can work together? Respect is the beginning of understanding. Understanding is the beginning of harmony. Don't limit yourself to groups with whom you are comfortable and familiar. The more you go outside the box to include others, the more your organization will grow. Now you may end up with an Iranian board member, investors, and volunteers who never would have found you otherwise.

This scenario would be just as true with any group in your community. In Fullerton, we have a Korean Christian church with more than six thousand participants. Since partnering with them, we have tripled our Korean participation and brought on new board members. Koreans make up 18 percent of our community and are generally an affluent population. So this new participation has been very important to our growth.

Service Clubs

Another important network is service clubs. You can use your first hundred days to be treated like the beautiful young debutante at her coming-out party. Service clubs are desperate for new members. Your interest in joining one will have them rolling out the red carpet for you. Go to lunches at Kiwanis, Lions, Elks, Rotary, and any other clubs in your area people invite you to attend. If nothing else, you will have a great time and meet great new people. The rules of courting are similar to those of a debutante:

1. If you attend any one club more than three times, they will be expecting more of a relationship. So don't go more than three times in one year unless you expect to join the club.
2. Make every club feel special. If you aren't going to join, the trouble is with you, not them. "The time doesn't work with my schedule" is always a great and true excuse for not joining.
3. Don't lead them on. If you aren't planning on joining, don't continue to give them hope you might join.

Most service clubs are aging. They don't have the young influx of people they used to have. For a non-profit leader, this isn't a bad thing. People in service clubs have a desire to serve the community, are very social people, are established in the community, and generally have very able pocketbooks. They love having younger members bring new life to the club, so you will be well received. If you go into a service club with the right attitude, you will enjoy it as much as they enjoy you. Most people join service clubs for the same reason as you: to network and help their business. But what they find once they spend time getting immersed in the club is that they really enjoy the work of making the community a better place through service projects. Service clubs are non-profits that focus on specific missions. Lions Clubs work to help the blind and Rotary works to end polio, for example. But all do local service projects in their community and invest much with organizations like yours.

Most service clubs started at the turn of the twentieth century, when the industrial revolution changed the world. People worked for the first time in large cities and large factories away from their hometowns and family and friends. There was a need to form bonds in their new situations, which they did with unions and clubs. As a new middle class emerged, there was a desire to have the feel of the leisure class who had country clubs and society clubs raising money for the poor in ways that, ironically, were filled with opulence and exclusivity. Service clubs abounded, fraternal orders that sometimes included rituals and great camaraderie. But after the communication age ramped up and every household had a phone and television, and the cultural revolutions of the 1960s started, the need to belong to such clubs started to deteriorate. Those born after 1950 saw these organizations as passé. Some clubs, however, that had a strong bent on service and maintained membership of many of the power players in the community continued to stay strong.

This is your job when courting service clubs: to

determine which club in your community has the strongest group of movers and shakers in its ranks. These are the clubs that thrive. Generally, these are the clubs that do the most for the community as well. Each community will be different. In some communities it will be a Lions Club that reigns supreme. In others it will be a Rotary Club. In others, Kiwanians will rule the day.

In my community of Fullerton, CA, the Rotary Club to which I belong has 160 members, including the heads of most industries, four former city councilmen, the police and fire chiefs, and the directors of most major non-profits. This club is only one of three Rotary Clubs in town, but it's by far the largest. By contrast, in a neighboring city, the Rotary Club has less than forty members, and the Kiwanis Club has the clout with former mayors and captains of industry. Every community is different.

If a club is doing well, it's usually for good reason. In our club's case, it's not just because of the power players in its membership, but also because it's a very fun club with very fun people and activities. I can honestly say that my Rotary meeting is often a highlight of my week. I can also say that I can directly attribute hundreds of thousands of fundraising dollars in the past four years to friendships I made in my Rotary Club.

Time Management

How will you have time for all these networks? I set aside my lunches Tuesday and Wednesday for networks, usually one breakfast each week, two fundraisers each month, and one after-work happy hour each month. That will generally do it. I'm not much of a drinker, or I would have more happy hours. If I played golf, I would certainly include that, but unfortunately the game never interested me. I have other lunches on Thursdays and Fridays with investors, board members, or people I meet in networks. None of these events are hard to do. They are all generally fun, some more fun than others. Once you become a regular at these events, the whole perception of you changes. You stop being an outsider. People start to tell you, "It seems as if you have always been here." People trust you. They enjoy your company.

Deeper Connections

With membership comes responsibility. You will be asked after a year or more to sit on boards and committees and take on responsibilities in your networks. Generally you can pick and choose the jobs you feel you can do well without feeling like a chore. My motto is if you enjoy everything you do, you will never feel stress doing it.

When the time comes to ask for things for your organization, you are no longer an outsider asking for money. Your organization is no longer a stranger. You are family asking for help. But this takes time to develop. Usually more than a hundred days. Right now you are sowing the seeds for the future.

I met an insurance agent through our chamber of

commerce in my first few months at the Muck. He saved
us thousands on our insurance. Then I got to know him
and his wife when I joined our Rotary Club. After a while
they become regulars at our events, and he became a
$500 sponsor my first year. A few months after that, he
introduced me to his friend who writes million-dollar
checks to the big hospitals and colleges in town. Then
he helped me get her interested in a project of mine.
Three months later she sent me a $50,000 check to fund
the whole project. The actual project was $5000, but she
was very old and heard $50,000. I did not correct her! So
we expanded the program to be a three-year, $50,000
program. If I had never joined chamber or Rotary, none
of that would have happened. That is networking.

Serving on Boards

Once you have networked the town to the point where
you feel like Norm from *Cheers*—everybody knows your
name, and they're always glad you came—you can see
if there is one strategic partnership that would really be
a game changer for your organization. It might be one
that both adds prestige and strengthens your reputation at the same time it serves your mission in a big
way. It would also be one in which you can help them
in some large way. You get to know the staff and board
at this potential partner and start a small partnership.
The courting process goes well, and you want more,
and you are helping them also. They ask you to sit on
their board. This is the time to say yes. You shouldn't

sit on many boards because you have your hands full with your own organization. Also, you can't raise money for more than one organization at a time. But this is a special case; what you do for them is important enough that they want you on their board. And what they do for you is big enough you want more access to them.

A great example of this in my career is our Fullerton Sister City Association. I became friends with the president of that organization, which focused entirely on cultural exchanges with junior high students going back and forth between countries. I proposed doing an art exhibit at the Muck between countries. It was very successful. I could see how an international art exhibit every year would add prestige to our cultural center and provide opportunity for our local artists to exhibit overseas. This is very important to build an artist's resume. I could also see how these were expensive exhibitions, and Sister City wanted to help support them. I joined the board. We started a new fundraiser at our center, which now raises thousands for Sister City, and half the money goes to fund our exhibitions. Through this partnership we have enhanced our mission, funding, and reputation. It's 20 percent of our exhibition calendar and funding each year now. We have taken exhibits to Korea, Japan, and Mexico. Sister City is also enhanced by having this new high-visibility program and fundraiser.

If you decide to become more deeply involved in a strategic partner, don't do it in your first year at an organization. Wait until you are settled and your course isn't only set but well on the way. Also, don't sit on more than one non-profit board at a time. I have made the mistake of sitting on multiple boards only to find that it pulled focus from the main organization I was hired to serve. Try to pick one that fits well with your mission, so your time there is really still working for your organization. Make sure the board of the partner is clear that you can't work as a fundraiser for them. If you are successful, they may assume you will help them be financially successful. You can help them with advice and joint fundraisers, but your duty is to your job first. In many cases it would be a conflict of interest to raise money for your partner's board while doing so for your own organization. Make sure that your organization's board is aware and in agreement with your serving the partner on their board.

Honing Your Skills

In terms of becoming great at networking and partnering, I would refer you to an oldie but a goodie. I have found that the best self-help book is the first self-help book. I make it required reading for my staff. *How To Win Friends And Influence People* by Dale Carnegie is a bit dated in its references, but it's the book that spawned the genre and is still the king. I find it to be the best at teaching the tricks and tips to have people eating out of your hand.

Review

1. The cornerstone of success as a non-profit director is strategic partnerships.
2. Create a resource map.
3. Once you have a map, go forth and network with non-profits, churches, service clubs, local businesses, and chambers of commerce.
4. Networks involve long hours but don't really feel like work if you enjoy people.
5. Networks can be virtual e-villages.
6. Expect that networks, where you get something from them, will require you to take on responsibilities and also give to them.

Now that you are on your way to being a world-class networker, we can talk about making these networks translate into funding for the mission of your organization.

Developing the Missionaries, Part III: Investors and Fundraising

Don't think of yourselves as fundraisers. Think of
yourselves as bridge builders. You are building a bridge
between people's need to invest in their community and
your mission that serves that community.
    —Mother Teresa (to her mission's board of trustees)

I confess. Mother Teresa didn't say that. I said that just now. I say that all the time. I thought if you heard it coming out of Mother Teresa's mouth, you might take it more seriously. It's true, however, that if you stop seeing fundraising as getting money for your cause and start seeing it as bringing people to your cause, you will be more successful. You are not some panhandler begging for money. You are not some pathetic thing guilting the more fortunate out of their money. You are an opportunity for truly responsible people to strengthen their community. A strong community helps everyone in it prosper.

Now that you are halfway through your first hundred days and spending the last fifty days networking, you will start to transform networks into investors. People who invest in their community have already made the decision that they want to give back; the only questions in their minds are "To whom?" and "How much?" These are people we have traditionally called "donors" in most non-profits because they donate money. In this book we have taken to calling them investors. An investor has a larger scope than a mere donor. An investor could be investing in the Three Ts—time, talent, or treasure. They could be volunteers, board members, financial supporters, or providers of in-kind goods and services. These are all equally important ways to invest. A donor is just giving money to an organization with nothing expected in return. That is a very shallow relationship, and I can't think of too many people who want to just give away money with no expectations.

No one ever raised large amounts of money by asking for large amounts of money. Money is raised when you connect people to the mission. More important, the mission is accomplished when you connect people to it. Money doesn't even need to be in the equation. This can happen only through networks and the strategic partnerships created, as we discussed in the previous chapter. In this chapter, we will discuss grant making, fundraisers, and social enterprise, with their myths and mysteries exposed.

Diversified Funding

It's important to have diversified funding. Most non-profits (with few exceptions) should have income from all these sources:

- Mission-based earned income
- Fundraisers
- A mix of individual, corporate, and government investors
- Grants and foundations
- Social enterprise
- Support groups
- In-kind income

Mission-Based Income

Mission-based income would be any earned income you get for doing your mission. Because we are doing a community service, it doesn't pay for the whole cost of the service. If it did, we would be a for-profit company, and only those with money could afford our services. There would be no public benefit. In the arts, mission-based earned income is ticket sales. In social service, it may be contracts paid to you for providing services. In medical non-profits, it could be reduced payment for services or contracts for research studies. But most non-profits have a way to generate at least some income from doing their mission.

For example, most Boys & Girls Clubs charge youth ten dollars a year for membership. This helps youth feel invested in the mission, but it's a minute percentage of what the programs cost. This would be mission-based income.

Fundraisers

How do you connect people to the mission? If you
ask this question, you are thinking in terms of LMV—
leading people to the mission and vision. Most people
don't do this. Think of a traditional non-profit looking
for donors. What do they do? They host a big, splashy
fundraiser, usually with an auction, a chicken dinner
that tastes like rubber, and a boring program with a
bad speaker asking people to give. It's usually done
in such a way that peer pressure kicks in and people
give big bucks to show off in front of their friends. In
many cases these are effective at raising thousands or
even hundreds of thousands of dollars. Or so it would
appear. But in reality, if you peek behind the curtain,
things are not what they seem. Many of the top bid-
ders are actually board members bidding up the price
on auction items and trying to get others to give in the
big ask. When the event is done, these board members
are not actually buying the items, or they are giving
what they have agreed to give as board dues. The
whole thing is a charade. Most of the real top donors
are giving not because of the fancy party but because
of some connection to the mission. They gave in a
check and didn't even go to the party half the time.
The people at the event are guests invited by board
members who were forced to buy and fill a table. Do
you think the people they invited are going to get a
real connection to the mission from this dinner? Others are with corporations who sponsored the event
because of some connection with the mission or some

perception this is important to their clientele. When you really dissect the event, they are marginally successful at raising money and are poor ways to connect people to the mission.

In the press you will read that the event raised $100,000 for the charity. But much of what gets reported are gross accounting figures. Once you take out food costs, rentals, fundraising costs, printing, mailing, money promised that is never delivered, and marketing the event, it may end up making 20 percent of the gross.

If you hire an outside fundraiser, it may even be less. Outside fundraisers range from very effective help to some who may be a poor fit or an outright scam. That's why using your network for references and mentorship if you are going to use an outside fundraiser is important. You will have to add all the event costs on top of their fees. They don't work on percentages and can actually lose money for an organization. I'm not saying they are bad. In some cases they can be a great asset, depending on their reputation and what they are hired to do. Before hiring an outside fundraiser, make sure they are capable and are contracted to do something you couldn't do without them.

Non-profit fundraising events have become a big industry for caterers, rental companies, professional fundraising consultants, event planning people, and hotel banquet rooms. But they don't always do a great deal for the non-profit they are designed to help. Most fundraising events lose money in their first few years of operation.[1] Many fundraisers are said to be "friend-raisers" because they bring people in the door more than money. But are they really connecting people to the mission?

For many years at the Muck, we put on a big gala event every year that took a whole year to plan, ate up valuable staff time, monopolized the board, and had large up-front costs. The gross was approximately $60,000 or more, and on a budget line, it looked very effective. This went on for decades. But when examining the event closer, we found it only netted $20,000 at the end of it all. What we realized upon a true assessment of the event was that our sponsors would sponsor anything we asked them to sponsor because they were connected to the mission. Our board members, who bought tables, would put that money into anything we asked them to buy because they were our board and were committed to us, not the fundraiser. Once we took the sponsors and board out of the fundraiser, we realized we were putting on the event for ourselves. No one was coming except the people board members invited to their tables. We were soliciting auction items and spending a year getting it together. At the auction we were buying the items ourselves. The whole event was a way for us to throw a party for ourselves and make ourselves feel good. It brought in very little new money or new investors, and it had no real connection to our mission. It was a very fun party.

1   *Association of Fundraising Professionals CFRE test prep*

I'm not putting down very fun parties. I love parties.
But if you decide to have a large annual fundraising
event or plan to tweak the one you have, ask yourself
these five questions:

- How does it connect people to the mission of the
  organization?
- Is it a strong connection?
- How does it help with our strategic goals and vision?
- Does it bring in new potential investors?
- Is this the first experience you want for new investors
  of the organization?

The Muck went through many evolutions of our fundraising events in the first five years of my tenure. When
I started we had one event only—an antique car show
with a gala dinner attached. It became evident that the
people throwing the dinner and the people organizing
the car show were not the same group. They didn't have
the same interests and didn't even get along very well.
The car show people perceived the gala organizers as
interlopers in their car show. People coming to the gala
were a different crowd. So it felt as if a fancy dinner had
broken out in the middle of the car show.

In the second year we moved the dinner to a second,
stand-alone event in the fall while the car show was in
the spring. We combined the dinner with a Halloween
party a local sponsor wanted to throw and made it
a masquerade ball. Now instead of the one big event
raising $20,000, the two events each raised $20,000. Our

fundraising doubled. We hoped the ball would grow each year, but after three years, it was still only generating $20,000. That was when we did a true assessment of what was going on. The two events basically broke even on costs, tickets, auction, and bar. The money raised came from sponsorship. We asked the sponsors if they would continue to support us if we dumped these events and did something else. They all said yes except one, who was moving on anyway. That sponsor's owner had a brush with cancer and was diverting all his giving to cancer charities. Many of our new sponsors had come in to sponsor programs rather than the fundraiser anyway. Our board said they would support at the same level regardless of what we did. So we had an epiphany that even if we didn't do either of these events, we would still make the $20,000 each year from our sponsors as long as we did something.

So we started year four with a clean slate. The car show committee took this finding as a challenge. They decided they liked doing the car show and wanted to continue it and see if they couldn't grow it. The gala committee decided to fold and work with me on new fundraisers that went with our mission. We asked ourselves the five questions. We decided to have two new fundraisers that were more in line with our mission. Since we were a cultural center and our mission was the arts, why not have arts-based events? We were always trying to get people to come to see our concerts, classes, and gallery. Why not make a concert or festival our fundraiser?

We started an Arts Legacy Award event, in which

we give an award to someone in the community who has made a lifetime achievement in the arts. Usually they are founders of non-profits. We get their group to work with us on the event and help them raise money as well. We also started a luau dinner and concert. Both events now run with much less effort and involvement, as they are part of our normal concert operations. The two still make approximately $20,000 a year, as the ball did before. But they have brought in more investors and sponsors for other parts of our mission with much less effort. They tend to get more press and community attention. Next year the awards ceremony will become part of a larger folk music festival that has the potential to grow very large and still be part of our mission. We are looking at selling four thousand tickets, for a gross potential of $150,000 and net potential of approximately $70,000. The car show committee has not been able to grow as they thought and are calling it quits after this year's event unless new blood takes up the torch.

The interesting thing about fundraising events is that most organizations spend 60–80 percent of their fundraising efforts on these events, which usually generate less than 20 percent of their income. There are so many more effective ways to work. In our organization, we spent 60 percent or more of our time on fundraisers that generated 5 percent of our income five years ago, when we had a $430,000 budget. Now we have almost a million-dollar budget and spend less than 10 percent of our efforts on fundraisers, which generate 10 percent of our budget. Another 30 percent of our budget comes from our social enterprise, 20 percent comes from grants, 5 percent from corporate sponsorship, 5 percent from individual donations, and the other 30 percent from contracts and ticket sales in serving our mission. This is incredible, given that when I started, all our income came from three sources—a single fundraiser, a city sponsorship, and our social enterprise. In the past five years, our city sponsorship was cut in half, and we lost $60,000. Our social enterprise was in threat of being cut out. Without diversified funding sources, we would have gone under with either cut.

Individual, Corporate and Government Investors

Individual and corporate investors are those people who believe in your mission enough to financially invest in it. Individuals might include board members, people who pay membership fees, wealthy investors who fund a program you do, or those who contribute when you pass the hat or set up donation boxes at events.

Corporate investors would be companies who believe in your mission and want to fund you, your fundraiser, or one of your programs. They may also be companies you are invested in such as your bank, insurance company, or printer. As you are a major client, it makes sense that they invest in you. If you give a great deal of accounts to these businesses and they are not invested in you, you might want to shop your accounts to others who would invest in you. The corporate sponsor might also have a VP on your board, be part of your chamber or service club network, or feel your clients are their clients and do it purely for marketing.

Government investors would be the city or government entity who gives you an annual stipend without a grant because you do important work for the community or you do a service that they would have to do. If you have a contract with them to do services on behalf of the city, they may fall under earned mission-based income instead.

Grants and Foundations

Grant and foundation support comes from both grants you write for programs and foundations who support you without a grant. A foundation might provide support because one of its officers serves on your board, because they are a service club foundation in your network, or because they have a similar mission and give you an annual stipend without a grant.

I could write another entire book just on grants. I love them. I love writing them. I love getting them. I love the whole process. Grant writing is just a micro-form of strategic planning for one project or program. The process allows you to really plan a project out and see how it works with your mission and goals. A grant application lets you dream a program before it happens and study it. It allows you to really make sure it's viable. It's fun to dream and see if your dreams and vision can become reality.

Many people are afraid of grant writing or think it's

some grand skill that is far beyond them. However, grant
writing is simply proposal writing combined with the
strategic planning process.

The Five *Ws* and the Four *Hs*

Grant funders are looking for the LMV—the leadership,
mission, and vision—in every grant. If you can answer
the five *Ws* and the four *Hs* about your program in a
concise, passionate way while telling them about the
LMV, you can write grants.

What. What is the program? Make sure this is concise,
clear, and to the point. Don't muddy up the waters with
details about other programs or tangents that have little
to do with the program you are applying to fund. If they
give you three pages to talk about the program but you
can do it in one, then do it in one.

Who. Who is working on the program? Who is your
leadership for this program, and what are their creden-
tials? You will probably be asked to include resumes or
biographies of key personnel. Give details about who
the program is designed to serve.

Where. Where is your program being conducted? If it's
with a partner organization, why did you choose them?
Partnered programs tend to be more competitive. A
funder gets to see you working together in your community and fund two non-profits for the price of one.
This is always a plus with funders.

When. When is the program? When does it start and end each day, week, and month? What is the term of the grant? Does it fit within the timeline the grantmakers give in the guidelines? If you have space, provide a timeline of what happens when. This will help clarify things. For example:

- June: Program planned based on need and evaluation form past programs; grants written.
- November: Pre-production meeting with key personnel.
- January–March: Pilot expansion program is produced as per grant. Program runs M/W/F 3 p.m. to 7 p.m.
- April–May: Evaluation done on pilot program expansion.
- June: Final reports issued. Plans made for follow-up programs.

Why. This is your needs assessment. Now you have a chance to truck out the one you did in Chapter 3 and polish it off. You will rewrite it into a short paragraph or two fitting this program. Why do you do this program? Why is it important for the funder to fund this over the hundred other applicants? You have statistics, anecdotes, a compendium of evidence, and community support showing why this is crucial.

How. This is the nitty-gritty details of the program spelled out in no uncertain terms. How does it address your mission and goals with great leadership (LMV)?

How Much. This is the budget for the program with income from various sources, usually including a match for grant money and expenses highlighting the costs for the program. Always show where matching income is coming from and whether or not it's pending or received. It may be from another grant, a fundraiser, a sponsor, or general fund money. Always include 10 percent for administration costs but never more or less unless spelled out in the grant guidelines. Ten percent administration is considered standard for grants. Therefore if you are applying for a $10,000 match for a $20,000 program, your expenses would show 10 percent administration costs with half ($1000) coming from the grant. There should be a column for the total costs and a column for the grant funds. Income and expenses should always balance out.

A simple sample budget can be seen in the table.

How Well. How will you evaluate how well you have achieved your goals with this program? Funders want to know the program will be evaluated at the start, middle, and end of the program period.

How Long. If this isn't a one-time need, how will this program be sustained after the funding is gone? Funders want to know that they are not funding something great that just dies the year after because there was no plan in place to sustain it.

Grants usually have their own forms. Some are better written than others. It may be hard to get the five *W*s

INCOME	Match	This Request	Total Budget
From Fundraiser	$5,000 (Received)		$5,000
From Federal Grant	$5,000 (Received)		$5,000
This Request		$10,000 (Pending)	$10,000
TOTAL INCOME			**$20,000**
EXPENSE	**Match**	**This Request**	**Total Budget**
Salaries	$5,000	$7,000	$12,000
Marketing	$2,000		$2,000
Materials	$2,000	$2,000	$4,000
Administration	1,000	1,000	$2,000
TOTAL EXPENSES	**$10,000**	**$10,000**	**$20,000**

Figure 1. *A simple, sample budget.*

and four *H*s in to their form. But your grant depends on a clear, concise plan for your project with a track record of doing this and a reasonable budget.

Before you start writing one word, make sure you check over the grant guidelines. Make certain you are eligible for the grant. Make certain you write it the way they want it written. And make sure your project will be competitive. There is no sense writing a grant for a project that is marginally acceptable when you are competing against many strong proposals. This is a mistake many organizations make. They hire a grant writer who is happy to get paid for writing a grant application that he or she knows unlikely to be funded. It's not your grant writer's responsibility to tell you if you are competitive unless you ask. Grant writers will do what you ask of them. If you hire a plumber and tell him you want all new pipes, he's not going to tell you, "You don't need them." That's money to him. Sure, you can use new pipes, but that's not the same question as whether you need them. You must take an honest look at the guidelines and ask yourself if you are competitive for this grant. "Are you competitive?" is a different question than "Are you eligible?"

If you are writing for an after-school program serving children ages twelve to eighteen and most of your kids are older, but the grant serves five to twelve year olds, you are eligible because you have twelve year olds. But you are probably not going to be competitive. It's acceptable and a good idea to call the funder and ask if your project would be competitive. Don't ask if you are eligible because they will say yes. But asking if you are competitive will tell them that you don't want to waste their time or yours. Calls like this also help forge a relationship with the funder. They will remember you when they are evaluating your grant. If you heeded their advice, they will remember that too.

If grant writing isn't your thing and your organization doesn't have an experienced grant writer, ask a partner organization for help. Maybe you can share a grant writer with another organization or contract it out. Just make sure your grant writer is covering all of these things and that the overall grant represents the mission, the goals, and key leadership on the project (LMV).

Keep in mind that most grants are received not just because of the proposal, but more often because of relationships forged. Once you have identified potential grants and funders, invite them to come for a site visit.

Seeing is believing. Forge relationships with funders. If they send you a survey, fill it out. If they email you, respond within twenty-four hours. (Our policy is to respond to all emails and phone calls within one business day.) If you are not responsive to them, they may not be as helpful to you. Call them with good questions and allow them to help you. This helps get them invested in your project.

Many times grants are decided by peer panels made up of people in your industry, usually other non-profit directors and board members. Several times I've received a very competitive grant I hadn't expect to get. Later I found out that one of my strategic partners or networking partners was on the panel. In grants, karma is very real and very instant. What you do and who you are in partnership will come back to you.

The best place to start finding grants and foundations that might support you would be with your resource mapping—making sure you identify grantors through Google searches, board members, and peer networks. If you are a social service charity, you should have a relationship with your local United Way. They are an umbrella for local charitable giving to social service networks.

All charities should have a relationship with their local community foundation. A community foundation is a pool of funds from local investors and endowments to be given out to local non-profits. It's designed for investors who want to give money without the work of managing it. For example, you might have a modest income and savings and in your will want to leave some money to charity for pets in your area. But you don't know any, so you would put in your will that you want the money to go to the community foundation for pet charities in your area. The community foundation would do the rest. When you pass on, they will make your gift part of an endowment for pet charities in your area. Your money does more good because it gets put into a larger pool, and you didn't have to do anything. They do the work for you.

Generally, these are the largest pools of funds in your area available for grants. A good relationship with them could mean a good relationship with all the funders in your area. They don't just give grants. They are also important in advising you and introducing you to their peers who are investors of non-profits. Invite the community foundation to a site visit and use them as mentors. In my experience they can be immeasurably helpful and supportive.

Social Enterprise

This is a relatively new concept in non-profits but a very important source of potential income. The term refers to business ventures that make money while doing good for communities. It's not just a non-profit idea. There are many companies getting rich on social enterprise, and there are college MBA degree programs in the subject. Think environmental companies in alternative energy, for example. Another would be nutritional organic food companies or locally sourced restaurants that give back a percentage of profits to the community they serve.

The secret to social enterprise for a non-profit is to ask yourself, "What do we have that other people would pay money to use?" Or to look at it another way, "What could we produce that would fit within our mission?" These are two different ways to approach social enterprise.

In the first, social enterprise isn't mission-based. For example, we run a cultural center in a beautiful historic building with almost nine acres of landscaped gardens. Our property is our best asset. So it was a no-brainer that my predecessor started a social enterprise, a wedding business to raise money for the arts programs.

The problems came in figuring out how to set it up and making sure the social enterprise didn't overshadow the mission. Our wedding business is handled by a caterer-partner who handles 100 percent of the business. We receive a site rental fee and a small percentage of the catering. But the weddings were taking over the schedule, becoming disruptive to neighbors, and causing some havoc on the historic house and grounds. We solved this problem with a new contract, better oversight, and stricter policies so that everyone knew what to expect and what the rules were. Within a year all problems ceased. If your social enterprise involves an outside partner, make sure you have a very good contract done with a lawyer, spelling out exactly what you want and expect. Now we have more control and money, with fewer problems and less time involved.

But you don't need a fancy historic building to have a social enterprise. In a previous art center, we were in a very poor inner-city area of Long Beach, Calif. It was not a place people were going to come for a wedding. It was fraught with gang problems, shootings, and drugs in the park around it. The center had a free program that allowed kids to graffiti art on our walls, but only if they stayed free of arrests for tagging. It was a very successful program and an important part of our mission. The walls became famous in the hip-hop community. We decided to use it as a social enterprise and allowed Hollywood film companies to use the site as a location for films in exchange for fees. In two years we had several projects filmed there, generating thousands of dollars for programs.

Some organizations might just have a nice space they can rent out for meetings when they aren't using it. Others might have a leader or staff member with great expertise in an issue. People could pay him or her to come and speak at events, he or she could do webinars, and the organization could host conferences. It might even generate enough money to pay his or her salary. It's important not to get so caught up in the fundraising that you let it interfere with the mission. If we cancel mission-based programs because we make more money from our wedding business, then the tail is wagging the dog. You must put parameters in place to control this. Don't be tempted by the money. Remember that the money is raised for the mission. We have had to say no to weddings that would raise $7,000 in one day so we could do a festival that lost money. But the festival was our mission, not the wedding.

In the other case of "What could we produce that would fit within our mission?" the social enterprise IS the mission, so there is no worry about interference. An example is Homeboy Industries. The king of this type of mission-based social enterprise is Father Greg Boyle, a Catholic priest who runs a shelter for ex-gang members in East Los Angeles. His clients tell him that they can't get jobs because of their prison record, and without jobs it's hard to stay out of gangs. Gangs provide work dealing drugs. So Father Boyle started Homeboy Industries. In the beginning it was just a T-shirt shop designing, printing, and selling T-shirts. The shirts became very popular. Then they started making shirts for other people and competing with other T-shirt screen printers. Next they started getting contracts to paint out graffiti. Then they started a bakery. They had some problems growing too fast but developed a great brand name in Homeboy Industries. They accomplished their mission of making jobs for their former gang members, jobs that made them proud.

Several women's shelters have started bakeries as well. Some homeless shelters have started temp employee firms. A foster care site in our community runs a coffee shop that is a job training and emancipation program for foster youth. The list is endless. All of these found a way of addressing the need of the non-profit by starting an actual business and using it as training and a resume builder for their clients.

At the Muck, we started a second social enterprise that is mission based. We have great arts education programs that are compliant with the California state standards for schools. Over the past few years, schools have been closing down their arts programs with budget cuts and new laws restricting them. We offer a program that allows them to reinstate arts at a lower cost with our artists-in-residence. Since promoting this program, we have increased arts education 800 percent, and it has gone from 5 percent to 30 percent of our income. But more importantly, we are keeping arts programs in schools that would have cut them and helping employ artists and art teachers in our community.

Social enterprises that are mission-based can't fail because even if the business doesn't succeed, just the act of doing it is a learning experience for the clients and so serves the mission. Therefore, even failure is part of the mission if they learn from it.

Support Groups

Support groups are very valuable but hard to start. It's much easier to take a dysfunctional support group and make it functional than to start one from scratch. Starting one has to be the idea of a volunteer or board member because in essence it starts an organization within an organization. If someone wants to do this, encourage it. Even if the attempt isn't successful, the person is mission building, showing leadership, and enhancing the vision. He or she may fail in starting a group but succeed in bringing new investors into the organization. Share your resources and mentor people in their organizational and managerial skills.

If the support group exists but is dysfunctional, you can use the same LMV principals we have been discussing to restore them to a functional group. Teach their leaders what you have learned as a leader, and they may come around. These support group leaders are your future board members and investors, so treat them well.

The key to working with support groups is they are generally older and set in their ways. They were doing this long before you came along. They have underwear older than you. The organization may have made you their leader, but the support group didn't. All you can do is help where help is wanted, give advice when asked, and subtly try to influence them to make good choices as a mini-organization within your organization. If you are successful, you will have led them without them even knowing it. But if they don't want your help or advice, you must walk the fine line of showing them respect for their service and investment without committing a great deal of staff, money, and resources into their project, which could be a sinking ship.

At the Muck, I inherited two support groups. The Center Circle is a group of housewives, artists, and teachers who started the support group in 1968 when they were in their thirties and forties. Now they are in their seventies and eighties but still plugging along. They have been affected by attrition, mostly due to the deaths of members or their retiring out of town. When

I started they were on the verge of giving up and closing down. We worked together to revitalize their mission, recruit new leaders and members, and find new sources for them to assist the organization. Now their ranks are back up near 150 after recruiting early retirees, which brought new life into the organization. They are making money for the organization and enjoying their renaissance under renewed leadership.

By contrast, the mostly male car show committee resisted change, even though they suffer from the same issues. They maintain the status quo. They are considering closing down after next year's event. Even though we disagree on how to grow the event and their efforts are waning, they provided a great fundraiser for the organization for almost twenty years and kept it afloat when this fundraiser was all the organization had. For that I am grateful. I can't be angry because they don't want to follow my suggestions. And they appreciate my respect and support even though we disagree on management issues. When the fundraiser ends, we will not part, and there will be no animosity either way. They will continue to be investors, and the fundraiser will end its run with great love and respect.

Muck board members want to start new fundraising events all the time. That is a sign of passion for the mission and a great board. But we have come up with ways that keep new ideas from sucking up valuable resources. When board members get the urge to lead a new fundraiser or program, we have a policy agreement that they can't use staff resources for it except the day of the event, and they can't use the organization's money to fund it. They must find new sources of funds to make it happen, not use existing sources or tap current investors. If they agree to that, they can try anything they want. With this agreement in place, we have three different board-generated committees/projects underway, including a very successful jazz festival.

In-Kind

The most underrepresented piece of the fundraising pie is in-kind investments. The organization gets something free for which it would normally pay. Common in-kind investments we have received include a van, a copy machine, printing services, legal services, accounting services, and web design services.

Some non-profits do not list any of their in-kind investments in reports or budgets. Others list everything right down to every volunteer hour. There is no wrong way. You just want to be sure that everything you list on your budget is properly accounted for and can be tracked and backed up with paperwork. Therefore, if you list volunteer hours at ten dollars an hour, make sure you have a sign-in sheet tracking every hour. If you list a legal service, make sure there is a letter to the lawyer thanking him or her for the service and noting that the normal fee of $150 an hour has been waived for five hours of reviewing your contracts. Now when your budget shows you received $750 in legal services, you have paperwork to justify that with auditors. When reflecting in-kind goods and services in the budget, you must be sure it's reflected both in income and expense. If you get free printing in the amount of $500 donated to print postcards for your event, you would put it as an expense in marketing and reflect it in income. Most people keep in-kind as separate lines in their budgets because some funders may not consider it actual income. By keeping it as a separate line item, it's easier to decide when you must include it in a budget report to a funder. Other funders love in-kind, and some will allow you to use it as matching funds for grants. That might save you $10,000 or more getting matching funds for a grant project. The more you can match, the more you can ask for programs.

Attracting Investors

Now that you understand the complexities of income and ways to report it, let us return to how you capture it in the first place. You must have an investor's packet. This should be both a physical brochure and an online PDF that can be downloaded from your website. You want them to know more, so don't make it overly complex or wordy. The investor's packet should include the following:

- great pictures and visuals
- a few items from your needs assessment—a startling fact, great statistic, warm anecdote, or testimonial
- your mission statement—it should send the message

that you are a newly revived organization with a mission and goals that you know how to reach
- bullet points stating what's in it for them. What do they get from helping you? Exposure? Recognition?
- a list of the many ways they can contribute and what those contributions do.

Remember, you are not asking for money. You are asking for scholarships, a new computer lab, or a new dance series. It should invite them to come take a tour, to meet with you and see your great new strategic plan. This brochure will just reinforce the impression they already have of you. Once they are interested, here are my LMV commandments for raising funds:

Connect the investors to the mission first. Invite potential investors to take a tour and see firsthand the amazing feats you are performing at your organization. Thanks to your deft leadership, they have been hearing about your work in networks and from friends. Show them firsthand what you do and dazzle them. Having a set and rehearsed tour that dazzles with your staff is always a huge plus. Having a way they can "tour" you by website and mobile device is now as important as the physical space. Make sure your web presence connects people to the mission. A good tour drives more fundraising than any rubber chicken dinner gala.

Never just ask for money. You are building mission. You are building programs. You are building bridges between those programs, goals, and mission on one shore; and the investor looking to help the community is on the other. If you concentrate on what you need and ask for that, rather than its cost, you will be more successful. "It costs $500 to put one kid through our program on scholarship. My goal is to have thirty new kids on scholarship next year. That's 30 percent of our program, and having a hundred teens in the program, by our calculations that would mean we are reaching 55 percent of the affected ninth graders in this school who are not yet committed to gangs. Is this something you want to help with?"

Offer options. There are many ways people can invest. There are multiple programs. They can give time, talent, or treasure. They can give to many programs or your fundraisers, capital campaigns, corporate sponsorship, or endowment. They have many options, each with its own benefits of investment. If you provide a smorgasbord for investors, they are more likely to eat at your establishment instead of patronizing the next non-profit down the road.

Thank investors. Investors who don't feel appreciated will rarely stick around. Make sure that your thank-you is in proportion to their gift. If it's a large gift, give them a nice present that is inexpensive but thoughtful and connected to the mission. If you give an expensive gift, you are telling them you didn't need their money. We often give gifts made by our artists with the Muck as the subject matter so that every time they see it, they are reminded about us and our mission.

Keep in touch. Thank-you cards and all correspondence should be imprinted with your brand. You should thank them even if it was just for taking a tour. After thanking them, put them on your membership list so they receive your brochures, reports, letters, and so on. If they are a large investor, take time to regularly invite them personally to events, or just out to lunch. It's important to know when a small- or mid-sized investor has the potential to become a larger investor. Keeping accurate databases helps track current and potential investors.

In late October or early November, you should send out an annual appeal letter to all investors with a clear, concise synopsis of the successes and challenges of the year followed by an ask for a pressing need or needs. It should be positive and upbeat, basically stating, "Look what we have done with your support," followed by "Here's what we can do with a little more help." The letter shouldn't be more than a few paragraphs and can include pictures or graphics. It should end with "Help us make next year an even better year..." with a final punch at your goal.

Strategic partnership is a key element of fundraising. Good partnerships can lead to sharing investors, mailing lists, fundraisers, and staff. If an arts non-profit decides to partner with a social service non-profit like a shelter, neither has anything to lose by working together. An investor isn't going to say, "I want to support the arts, not the shelter anymore!" They are apples and oranges. The investor might like the fact they are working together for the community and start supporting both over another charity who doesn't partner. Many funders are now making partnership a priority in funding. We at the Muck started an arts program at a shelter and brought the funders out to see it. They were so impressed that not only did they give us an extra $40,000 to continue the program, but gave the shelter $15,000 to do more work on their own. The shelter's partnership with us not only brought in a large new program free to them, but generated $15,000 additional funding for their core programs.

Diversify fundraising. Don't have too many funds in too few baskets. If a major investor pulls out, you will be caught in the lurch. It could mean your demise. Make sure you have many streams of income (as we discussed earlier) and many investors.

Have great programs. If your staff and programs are truly serving the community, word will get out. Instead of one development director talking about your organization, everyone in town will be talking about your organization and the amazing transformations that have happened there. A day doesn't go by in my town when someone doesn't walk up to me at a meeting or grocery store and say, "It's amazing what you have done over there with the Muck!" My response is always, "I'm just the face of the Muck. There are approximately six hundred people working to make our place happen. I can't take the credit. But when are we going to get you involved?" They have already opened the door for me to invite them for a tour or ask them how they can help.

Market your mission. If people know about the changes going on in your organization, they will get on the train. Sun Tzu said, "When water can move boulders it's because of momentum." It's marketing that builds momentum. More on that in the next chapter.

Take care of the mission, and the funds take care of themselves. If you are leading your organization as we have discussed in this book, with the mission as job one and with well-defined vision and goals, you will only need to cash the checks and start new programs to better serve. People in your community are looking for well-run non-profits in which to invest. When yours starts getting noticed because of all you are doing right, half the fundraising burden is off of you. Every conversation revolves around the mission. Your name and face become synonymous with the organization and mission. Every person you meet is a past, present, or potential investor. Your staff is well trained in handling new investors. When this happens, you just have to decide when they walk in the door if they fit in time, talent, or treasure.

Review

1. Make sure you have diversified funding in at least most if not all of these categories:
   a. Mission-based earned income
   b. Fundraisers
   c. Individual, corporate, and government investors
   d. Grants and foundations
   e. Social enterprise
   f. Support groups
   g. In-kind income
2. Connect investors to the mission first.
3. Build bridges among those programs, goals, and mission on one shore; and the investor looking to help the community on the other.
4. Offer multiple ways people can invest.
5. Thank investors appropriately.
6. Correspond frequently with your investors.
7. Pursuing strategic partnership is key to fundraising.
8. Diversify fundraising.
9. Have great programs.
10. Market your mission.
11. Take care of the mission, and the funds take care of themselves.

Now that you are halfway through your first hundred days with everyone behind your mission and vision, including your investors, you must move the message out into the community beyond just preaching it. That is where marketing comes into play.

Spreading the Good News:
Marketing and Public Relations

Chapter 8

He said to them, "Go into all the world and preach the good news to all creation."

—Mark 16:15

Marketing is defined as the act of buying and selling in the market. In this case, we are buying and selling community investment in the form of our programs. This should be an easy sale if we have great programs that address important needs and if we really believe in them.

Like a church, non-profits grow through evangelizing the mission. Social media, websites, and newsletters are not goals but tools to getting out the mission and programs. Grassroots campaigns are the most effective strategy for success, and they're easier than ever to implement with new technologies.

First let's look at a history of successful marketing of non-profits. Churches were the first non-profits. The Jewish religion held together the twelve tribes of Israel by marketing its stories of a proud clan who escaped bondage. Most tribes and ancient religions are bound by stories, creation myths, and legends of great warriors and events that make the tribe proud. Hinduism is another ancient religion with great myths and legends. Modern religions are often started as reform movements. Christianity was a reform of Judaism in that Christ preached a new way to look at the Jewish faith, rebelling against the corruption that existed in the temples with the Pharisees. Remember that the Jews of Jesus's time were also under occupation by the Romans. Many religions are the product of oppressive regimes and corrupt officials. The Protestants protested corruption in the Catholic Church. Buddhism came from a reformation of Hinduism at first and spread through Asia at a time when oppressive emperors ruled. Generally a movement comes from crisis or oppression.

The same is true of non-profits. They usually start and spread in response to a crisis or oppression. The Red Cross came as a result the American Civil War. The Salvation Army started as a result of "Christian" groups ostracizing the poor in England. The March of Dimes sprang up because of the polio epidemic; this organization is on the path to wiping out polio in the world. Boys Clubs were an answer to the large number of orphaned and poor boys roaming the streets as delinquents in epidemic proportions. The AIDS epidemic ushered in a host of non-profits to deal with that disease's effects.

Let's look at the Salvation Army's marketing

strategy—it's among the most dramatic success stories for growing an organization. William Booth founded The Christian Mission on London's East side in 1865. As a minister, Booth hated the modern-day Pharisees in his own Methodist congregations who shunned the poor and criminals in direct opposition to Christ's teachings. He started a Christian mission in the lower socioeconomic neighborhood of East London with little success. They provided the three Ss—Soup, Soap, and Salvation. But they had trouble getting followers until they decided to become the Salvation Army, modeled after the military. New recruits received uniforms, a rank, and a mission. Now former criminals and the poor were no longer criminals and poor people—they had a new identity, a rank, and a mission to spread the Good News. They served in a force for good. In 1867, Booth had ten full-time workers, but by 1874, the number had grown to one thousand volunteers in forty-two countries in Christ's Army. In twenty years, he had built a worldwide movement. This is marketing and public relations.

It was the transformative quality that made Booth so successful. Prostitutes, drunks, and thieves became sergeants and majors in God's army. He gave people purpose and mission in a very literal and immediate way. Most non-profits from the eighteenth century until the 1950s wore uniforms and had some paramilitary organization to them. This helped people feel the mission and their importance in it. After the counter-cultural revolutions of the 1960s and 1970s, uniforms became passé. Organizations wanted to be less authoritative, and showcasing the mission became more about harmony and friendship. "Marches for a Cure" became "Walks" or "Runs for a Cure." By the 1980s, corporate emphasis on profit infiltrated non-profits, and former "boards of trustees" became "boards of directors." Mission was de-emphasized.

I'm not suggesting we go back to a time when everyone wore military uniforms. But I am suggesting that when we emphasize LMV, we win. The modern-day uniform could be T-shirts or polo shirts with your logo on it. And when people at your organization have a specially designed shirt with your logo—and they are clamoring to wear it—that is when you know your leadership is working and your mission is a source of pride with stakeholders. But it also helps to have a great, simple logo.

Your Logo

A logo should be a simple design that will be easy to read in grayscale or color. It should be bold, simple, and sharp enough that it can be easily read at a distance. It should, if possible, say something about your mission, even if only subtly. Think of great corporate logos that do this: the McDonald's golden arches is both a monogram and a nod to their history; the Nike swoosh says they are modern and moving forward; Audi's four circles represent the four historic German car companies that joined forces to create Audi.

At the Muck we used a historic M monogram from

the Muckenthaler's historical artifacts to create our logo. It's a craftsman-era typeface and just with one M shows our connection to history as a Historic Registry building and the Arts and Crafts movement. We sell monogrammed clothing with our logo in the gift shop. One investor paid more than $100 to have a custom sweater made for him with our logo on it.

Spreading the Word

Successful promotion of a grassroots non-profit organization follows the same guidelines as the evangelical promotion of a religion:

- You need apostles to spread the gospel.
- You need a great gospel for them to spread—a statement of the mission, stats on your program, stories of your triumphs, and legends of your heroes.
- You need miracles that have been worked and stories of the miracle workers. The people you helped have to be changed significantly enough that they want to tell others of your good works.
- You need rituals that keep people connected to the mission. These could be events, meetings, or lectures, but they must be interesting, involving, and regular.

Having these things in place is more important than any ads in newspapers or commercials on TV for promoting your organization.

///

Marketing Top Ten

Here are the ten commandments of marketing your mission in the community:

1. **Wear thy mission.** Stakeholders regularly wear clothing that represents the organization in a positive way.
2. **Thou shalt brand everything.** Put your name, logo, and mission statement on everything you do, say, or write. Letterhead, note cards, thank-you cards, brochures, uniforms, websites, emails, and envelopes are just some of the places that should shout, "We are here." Having a catchy nickname or acronym doesn't hurt if your name is long or hard to remember. We branded "the Muck" for Muckenthaler very successfully. We can't keep our T-shirts on the shelf because they say "What The Muck?" with "TheMuck.org" under it. People love them. Need I say more?
3. **Know thy mission.** Your mission statement and goals are prominently displayed at your organization, in all printed materials, in your web presence, and in the minds and on the lips of stakeholders.
4. **Stakeholders shall embrace networking.** They never show up at a networking event without branded items to give out, preferably a brochure on the organization. They have a great working knowledge of the organization, as well as its programs, mission, and goals. They always show up fifteen to thirty minutes early to network before the event

starts. Their goal is to invite people to tour your organization online or in person. This is the first step to getting involved. Look what Christianity did with just twelve apostles to start.

5. **Thou shalt show off thy mission.** The organization and you have a mechanism in place to host regular organized tours with staff. There are materials available in the tour detailing how people can invest in your mission and organization as volunteers, contributing special skills you need or financially helping support programs. You host booths at local events.

6. **Thou shalt have a written ask for help.** Brochures should have a wish list of what you need in terms of volunteers, special talents, and financial commitments. This could be, "We need volunteer tutors from 3 to 7 p.m. every weekday; we need business mentors willing to take youth interns; and/or $100 sends a youth to our business development program for a month." You should have a great web presence that matches your great brochure.

7. **Thou shalt have ritual celebrations of thy mission.** People are invited to regular programs that showcase the mission, such as performances, open houses, lectures, or inspirational stories of your alumni. People should feel as deeply about your non-profit as they would about their religion in the way it touches their lives. Develop a ritual with these events. Ritual brings a sense of importance and belonging. In our case, this is easy because we

host regular concerts, gallery openings, and festivals. But I start each event with a ritual opening in which I yell out, "Hello, Fullerton!" The audience has taken to yelling back "Hello Zoot!" We have ritual events within each event that people have come to expect. We have become a ritual part of their lives.

8. **Thou shalt partner strategically to spread the gospel.** Use your networks to create strategic partnerships in marketing, such as cross-marketing with partners. Put ads in their newsletters or programs, and they will do the same in yours. Buy ad space together to advertise a joint project. Share marketing staff or a street marketing team that distributes post cards on your organizations in local business districts or gathering spots.

9. **Apostles shall keep epistles.** You communicate with your flock regularly through email, mailings, newsletters, invites, postcards, and brochures to keep them informed on the progress of the mission. Your supporters regularly blog about your organization and post things on Facebook, Twitter, or other social media.

10. **Thou shalt handle thy publicity.** Keep on top of what is said about you in the media and generate regular press releases.

Advertisements

Notice that nowhere in this chapter do I suggest you should go out and buy a bunch of ads in the media.

Ads are the most expensive and least effective way to promote something as the primary source. It's often said that people must see something three times before they take notice of it. Ads are what you do when you have been well saturated into the community and you can afford to do this as an extra way to get noticed. It's never the primary way to start and should be considered only when budgets allow for it and the organization is quite successful.

Booths

Having a booth within a community event such as a festival, farmer's market, or holiday event is another great way to network and promote your organization. Generally, booths can be secured for $25–$200, depending on the event, expected attendance, and organizer. Sometimes you can barter for booth space. If the event brings ten thousand people to a community festival, you have the power to interact with ten thousand for a very low price. Unlike an ad, a booth is immediate and allows you to have a conversation with a prospective investor, volunteer, or client. We have found having booth space around town to be an excellent tool for promoting our organization. Decorate your booth with things that prominently display the mission. Compelling pictures of programs, your logo, and brochures might be a good start. If you can, provide a fun activity or giveaway from your booth that might bring people in. A giant fish bowl of candy always brings people to your booth.

Brochures

Your biggest promotional tool will be your brochure.
Make sure your brochure is well designed and quality
printed and is a great speaking tool for your organization. There is a misconception that brochures are
expensive to produce. They are not when you buy them
in bulk, and you will need a lot. Always get three bids,
and check discount printers versus local printers for
discounts. Prices vary widely. Your brochure should
showcase your logo, name, mission statement, organization history, key programs, and possible key goals. It
should make someone who sees it say, "I want to tour
this place," or "I want to find out more about this place."
Do NOT skimp on your brochure. This, your stakeholders themselves, and your website are the most important tools you must market. You should make them the
highest priority in terms of quality. A poorly designed
brochure reflects a poorly managed organization.

That doesn't mean you must spend a great deal of
money. At the Muck when I started, we spent $10,000
a year in marketing, mostly on ads, and no one was
coming in the doors. For our performing arts series, we
had a approximately five hundred people in the audience the whole season. While the former director spent
thousands on ads, the brochure was a series of Xeroxed
sheets of paper with no pictures in black and white.
We put together a new season brochure with staff. We
recruited design student interns from the local univer-
sity for the brochure. We used a volume printer until
a local printer offered to give us discounted printing.

Marketing students formed a street marketing team and distribute the brochures at local restaurants and hotels. Our stakeholders gave them out all over town. The next year we cut our marketing budget in half. Thirty thousand brochures were distributed. Our audience went from five hundred to over five thousand in one year. This past year we had over eleven thousand in our audience using the same methods.

Electronic Marketing

To further bring people to us, we revamped our website and started an e-marketing campaign. Electronic marketing is quickly becoming the most important and cheapest form of marketing. People now can see your organization on a bumper sticker and use the website URL or a QR code to look you up instantly on their phone. In the space of a minute they can learn about you, buy tickets to an event, donate money, or buy some of your merchandise. The patron can then forward the email to thousands of friends who can repeat the whole process. And at the end of the day you can track all this web traffic; new investors can be added automatically to databases; thank-you letters and invites to your next event can be generated automatically; and with little staff effort, you have just grown.

Creating ritual with your stakeholders is key to your web presence. This is done by regular weekly updates to your website; daily updates to social media like Facebook, YouTube, and Twitter; and weekly e-blasts to your flock. An e-blast is an email that goes out to everyone. You do not want to send one out daily or you become "spam" and people will unsubscribe. But a weekly email with interesting things such as contests, event invites, and surveys can keep the faithful engaged.

All these things take great hardware and software and a person or persons who understand it to program it all. It doesn't have to be expensive. A good Internet connection and a good computer in the hands of a savvy, web-experienced marketing staff member can get much of this done at the starter level for free or for cheap. As you grow so will the costs, but then you can afford to grow.

I must confess this isn't my area of expertise. It doesn't have to be. Making sure someone on your staff has the expertise and listening to that person is all you need. Getting a second opinion or having a committee occasionally helps when something is complicated because they will check one another, and the best ideas will rise to the top. For the couple of thousand dollars you may spend in a year getting your web presence up and running, you will reap ten times that amount in new investment in your organization and its mission.

Publicity

Publicity is the way you control how the public sees your organization. It's different from marketing in that marketing is proactive and publicity is, half the time, reactive. It has been said that "All publicity is good."

That is completely true if you control it. If you do not keep in control of publicity, it can be disastrous.

Publicity involves sending timely press releases out for events and new programs, or at the end of major programs to announce a successful result. A press release has a standard format. Templates can be found online by the thousands. It will state the five *W*s and the four *H*s (who, what, when, where, why, how, how much, how well, how long) like a grant, but in one paragraph. It should be written like an article in a newspaper, with a compelling title and opening followed by the details. If it's compelling enough, it may get published as the article. As more and more media outlets lose reporters, they have taken to printing press releases verbatim. A press release should go out two weeks prior to small events. With large events they should go out six weeks, four weeks, and two weeks prior, with phone calls to follow up with media contacts you know well or should know well. If you are trying to get something into a large magazine, you may need to send it out twelve weeks in advance. When a reporter calls you back, remember this is free publicity and treat him or her with the same urgency you would a large investor. Do whatever you can to get the reporter involved. Once you become very successful, you will know because the reporters start calling you first and asking for a story.

The biggest concern for an organization is bad publicity. Personally, I think that is a misnomer. There is no such thing as bad publicity. There is only publicity you don't control. Once you control it, it's no longer bad. For example, if your organization is the subject of a scandal, deep budget cuts, or a former employee who is dragging you through the mud, you can reply in two ways. You can bury your head in the sand or you can organize a response. Those who look at publicity as bad tend to bury their heads and hope it goes away. But a true publicist will see negative publicity as an opportunity. No one in the media wants to publish stories about happy little organizations doing great work. They want to publish conflict because conflict sells. You will get more publicity from a scandal, budget cut, or disgruntled employee than a hundred years of harmony. If you control that publicity, you can raise awareness and spin it in a positive way. Nowadays we tend to think of spin as pundits on TV lying for their side. But spin doesn't have to be lies. Spin is simply turning a story around to the other point of view.

For example, an employee at your organization is caught doing drugs with a youth client. It comes out in the press. If you do nothing, your organization will be thought of as the place where staff do drugs with the kids. But instead you send out a press release and conduct interviews saying the staff member was promptly put on leave while an investigation goes forward; you provided counseling for the youth; an apology was sent out to all parents with an assurance that this will not be tolerated; you are cooperating with the police; and random drug testing was instituted with all staff. A few days later, you send a press release inviting press to a meeting with parents. Some of your supporters are encouraged to write opinion pieces in the local papers supporting your position. A few days later, the staff member is fired after an investigation. A few days after that, a new policy addresses this and states that employees will sign a drug-free workplace statement and will agree to random drug tests as part of their job. Then a story is released about a great staff member at your organization making a difference. In the release you tell the media to be fair and cover the good stories from your organization with the bad. Now the one story that was negative has become a series of stories that are positive showing you as the hero, not the villain, for taking appropriate actions. More people are aware of you than ever before.

In 2010, the Muck was threatened with $80,000 in budget cuts from the city. The city took the position that we had been so successful in the three years since I had started that the cut would not affect us. A few former board members who left before my tenure wrote opinion pieces in the local newspapers that we didn't really do anything of consequence and should be cut. A former employee wrote that we wasted money and didn't need it. Others said we only catered to the rich and didn't need the money. The press wanted our comments. Some on my board said we shouldn't antagonize the city and leave it alone. They wanted me to take it and ignore the press. The majority of the board sided with me that it was an opportunity to show what we have been doing. We put out a press release with our side of the story. The outpouring of support was immediate and gigantic. Within a week we had many articles and op-ed pieces supporting us. More than 120 people attended Fullerton's city council meeting to protest our cuts. Our Facebook presence grew to more than 1,100 followers. The city was inundated with letters on our behalf. Because of this, a more reasonable cut was negotiated, the city showed us new respect, a new membership campaign drove our membership from just under two hundred to more than eight hundred, and a new infusion of investment more than made up for the cuts. We ended with a record year in income.

Non-profits are born out of crisis and conflict. A well-managed conflict usually will help you more than it hurts you. If you do good work and truly serve the community, you have no reason to hide anything. Be transparent and honest, and the truth will prevail.

Review

1. Spread the word through apostles of the mission.
2. Use uniforms with staff and branding in all you do.
3. Train stakeholders to network with branded items to give out.
4. Have a mechanism in place to host regular organized tours with staff.
5. Have a great brochure and website.
6. Invite community members to regular programs that showcase the mission, such as performances, open houses, lectures, or inspirational stories of your alumni.

7. Make sure all stakeholders know your mission statement and goals.
8. Use regular email, mailings, newsletters, invites, postcards, and brochures to keep stakeholders informed on the progress of the mission.
9. Develop organizational rituals.
10. Focus on booths at community events, electronic marketing, and press releases rather than expensive ads until you are established. These are inexpensive ways to get the word out.
11. Use publicity of your events, whether good or bad, to your advantage.

The simple truth of marketing a grassroots organization is that it all comes down to S = LMV; Leadership with an emphasis on the mission and vision of the organization leads to success. That is true in fundraising. That is true in marketing. Fundraising and marketing are both successful when you sell the mission and the mission is a great one.

Programming Success

Chapter 9

Insanity is doing the same thing over and over again, expecting a different result.
—Albert Einstein

A small body of determined spirits fired by an unquench-
able faith in their mission can alter the course of history.
—Mahatma Gandhi

To be successful on a grand scale, you must light your stakeholders' spirits with an unquenchable faith in their mission. That's all. This is leadership, as we have discussed. You also must ensure they carry out that mission as defined by the group and not by their own agenda. That is where programs come in. Programs are the ships that carry your mission out to the community.

It's very hard for me to tell you in this book what makes a good program versus a bad one, since there are many types of non-profits with many programs serving many missions. What I can tell you is that successful programs have the following in common:

- They all serve the mission *substantially*.
- They are all led by great leaders.

- After outreach, they are filled to the capacity they are designed to serve through evaluation.
- They all have a vision and goals for managed growth (or conclusion if the program is designed to end when the need is addressed).
- They all eventually generate their own support due to their success and leadership.
- They are well documented.

Serving the Mission

Programs are a function of mission, not the other way around. A program could be the coolest program ever conceived, but if it doesn't further the mission in a significant way, it's a waste of time. People have come up with many excuses to justify programs that are failures in terms of mission, which is one reason why organizations fail. People might say of a fun fundraising event that generates little money and doesn't serve the mission directly, "Yes, it's not related to our mission and doesn't make money, but it's a good friend-raiser." This is an easy excuse to believe. But if it's not connecting those "friends" to the mission or raising money for the mission, what good is having these friends come?

Some non-profits spend lots of time and energy on a program that the staff think is great but that the clients it serves do not use. In this case you must either connect the client to the program or part with the program. I have seen non-profits that cling to a nonfunctioning program because there is funding for it. "If we revamp or dump the program, we will lose the funding." This is the logic. But if the program isn't serving people, then what are you really taking the funding to do? Are you just providing a job for staff and pretending to do something? Don't you think the funder would rather have you tell them the program was not effective and you are fixing it? It may take more funding to fix it, which is an opportunity to raise more funding while making a better program.

This is where LMV formula comes in handy yet again. Remember that little gem from Chapter 1, "Ask People Their Opinion"? If your clients are not attending your program, ask them how they would fix it. By asking them, you pull them into the process. Now they are going to want to attend your program because you are using their ideas. It becomes their program by consensus. And if your clients are among the key stakeholders in the room when you conduct your strategic plan, they will become leaders in the program to get the word out to others because it was their idea.

It's never too late to redesign programs or to scrap them and start over. Each program requires a mini-strategic plan designed for it with a staff goal to improve the program (it could be volunteers and/or staff running the program), a board goal of how the board will support it, and a financial goal of how you will pay for it.

Program Leadership
Since programs carry out the mission, and staff members carry out the program, the leader of this program

is paramount to its success. The key leader of a key program can be as important to an organization's success as
the CEO. Follow these rules.

**Have a good working relationship with the CEO to
be effective.** If the leader of a program can't get along
with the CEO, one has to go, and it won't be the CEO.
Sometimes good people have conflicts in personality.
They are too alike or too different. Don't be afraid to
make changes when a good staff member just can't get
along with you. If you have done everything you can to
make it work, part ways amicably and move on. This is
too important a position to let a bad relationship interfere. This is your mission! I have had to do this on several
occasions. It's never easy, and there are always repercussions. Doing nothing would have been worse.

**Have a great working relationship with the clients
they serve.** Leaders provide a service for clients. It's hard
not to be liked when providing a service for people.
Therefore, if clients don't like the leader, something is
very wrong. Usually that "something" comes down to
what Aretha Franklin sang best—RESPECT.

Have the ability to be organized and lead others.
Mentorship is important here. As the leader you have
the ability to mentor them to be leaders. If they resist
mentorship, they might not be the best people to lead.
This is part of succession planning too (see Chapter 11).
By finding and training leaders, you guarantee there will

be people who can succeed you when you are ready to move on.

Have a great attitude. Refer to Chapter 1 on leadership.

Capacity Building Your Program

Great programs don't start out great—there is trial and error. There is experimentation, listening to your clients, evaluation, tweaks, growing pains, mistakes, miscalculations, and bad theories that don't pan out. Growing your programs successfully usually means that you have made honest evaluations of your programs by talking with clients and staff at regular intervals and have fixed problems along the way. A program that never grew is a program that has never been evaluated properly.

Do you survey clients and ask them what works and what doesn't in the program? Do you do the same with staff and volunteers? Do you keep statistics on the program and study those stats to see trends? When something doesn't work as planned, do you investigate, evaluate, and find out why? As you will read more in depth in the next chapter, all of these things are part of evaluation and can help you improve not only the program but funding. Most investors want to see program evaluations before funding another year. Also, program evaluations give you ammunition in the form of statistics and facts for requesting more funding to change or expand a program.

Program Vision and Goals

As your organization created a vision for itself at a stake-holders' retreat, so should the program vision be formed. Host a meeting of program staff, volunteers, clients, and former clients to go over goals for the program. You might also invite executive staff like your directors of administration, programs, development, and marketing if they exist at your organization. Study past program evaluations and goals. In this meeting you are the facilitator for the program leader. Ask those at the meeting, "How can we improve this program?" Do a SWOT analysis. Establish an important staff goal and board support goal for the next year and a corresponding budget. Bring food to the meeting. It will be more productive.

If the program is designed to end when the need is addressed, decide on a transition to a new program that addresses another need of the mission. If the whole mission is addressed and you are out of work because you cured cancer, I'll see you on Oprah's network.

Program Funding

A good program idea is generally an easy sell for seed money. If you have a great needs assessment and program concept, people will invest. Investors tend to like the idea of seed money because the program becomes the baby they birthed. There is a great deal of pride in that. If you tell investors you want them to seed a program for free AIDS testing at local high schools, they may not bite. But if your needs assessment shows

AIDS has increased by 50 percent at local high schools and one out of twenty students is likely HIV positive and may be transmitting to others, and if your program is voluntary and done through the nurse's office and health classes and comes with increased HIV education in health classes, they may be more willing to pony up the funds.

If you have an established program with established investors, a new program is very exciting for one of them to shepherd. If you have an established program you are scrapping for a new program, that is also very exciting, especially if the investor considers it his or her idea to change direction. I have never had problems getting seed money for a good idea because it's so exciting to be part of a new venture.

Once a program gets its legs and is in the experimentation period, it's often right for grant funding. You have established a track record with the seed money. Now you want to take it to the next level. This is what grant makers get excited about. Unlike your organization's usual investors, grant makers don't know you well enough to trust you with seed money. But they love to help out organizations that have proved themselves with a track record of success. A three-year grant with matching funds from another grant or fundraiser will take you to the next stage. Your resource map, community foundation, and peer networks will help you find the right funders for your program.

Now that your program has worked out all the kinks and has become established in the community, people don't want to see it end. This is where a local foundation or local government might give you an annual stipend to continue the program. Or you could support it with an annual fundraiser now that people are familiar with it and what it does to help in the community. It might even spawn its own social enterprise. It might spin off into a newer, larger program, starting the whole cycle over again with seed money. Each step in the process is an opportunity to connect investors with the mission and be that bridge.

Now, remember those partners with whom you have been networking? Can they be strategic partners for programs? Do you have a space and there is a great program out there that needs a space or vice-versa? Do you have clients, and another program needs clients or vice versa? Partnerships can be a great way to fill program gaps or increase program participation.

Program Documentation

Some non-profits get so busy doing the program they forget to document it. I have been guilty of this myself. It's like going on a whale-watching boat, seeing the whale breach, and forgetting your camera. You can tell people about it, but you have no proof. With non-profit programs, proof equals funding. Nothing connects investors to the mission like great documentation of programs serving the community:

• Pictures on your website

- Videos on your YouTube channel
- Facebook postings of photos and video
- Thank-you letters from clients
- Tours of the program to investors
- Statistics, evaluations, and surveys from the program

Documentation should make it into your thank-you letters to investors, your annual reports, emails, website, social networks, and to your board on a regular basis. How much would it impact your organization to show pictures of an eight-year-old girl smiling while using your program, followed by a thank-you letter by her in crayon, followed by statistics showing that juvenile crime dropped 20 percent in the neighborhood while your program was running. Do you think that program will get funded again next year? You'd better believe it!

Cookie on a Mission

There are many examples of great programs turning around a non-profit and redefining it. Ever hear of Girl Scout Cookies? People wait every year for these treats. This is a great example of a mission-based program and social enterprise that redefined an organization. It was one of the first social enterprises and defined the term "bake sale." Back in 1917, five years after Juliette Gordon started Girl Scouts, the girls baked cookies in a high-school cafeteria, which taught them baking skills under adult supervision. By the 1920s they sold for twenty-five to thirty-five cents a dozen, and two thousand

Girl Scouts took part throughout Chicago. All over the country, Girl Scouts hosted bake sales. By the 1950s they were standardized and sold in three varieties, including the Thin Mints we all know and love. In selling, the girls learn to sell, handle money, and speak publicly. It's now the Girl Scouts' largest fundraiser and social enterprise, and it's still consistent with the mission. Even the boxes are designed to spread the mission of scouting. Selling the cookies raises awareness and recruits girls to scouting as much as it raises money.

Folk Finds

In my own career, I can think of many instances where a great program redefined an organization, but I will focus on a recent example. When I started at the Muck in 2007, in spite of a forty-two-year history, the center had no real identity in the community. It was often overshadowed by the seven colleges and eleven theatres that existed in the college town of Fullerton. In my first two years, we tried every type of program we could produce on every day of the week and evaluated them. Our findings were not at all what we had suspected. We had theorized based on audience surveys before we started that classical, theatre, and high-end arts programs would be the most successful. We guessed from local community support that choral concerts and vaudeville might also do well. What we found was that none of these did very well. However, every time we did an ethnic folk music or dance concert, it sold out. It didn't matter what

ethnic group we did, it always sold out. This was a complete surprise. We delved into this and discovered that
none of the colleges catered to ethnic music or dance,
and there was a real desire to see it. We found out there
were local folk support groups that bought group tickets
to these shows. We found we had a core group at the
Muck who also wanted to see them. And we discovered
that each ethnic concert brought with it its own distinct
audience, most of whom had never seen the Muck. This
was why they were selling so well.

We also found that Thursdays (not Fridays or Satur-
days) were our best attendance, followed by Sundays.
Evidence showed that there were too many Saturday
and Sunday events competing, whereas on Thursdays
there was an early evening farmer's market that brought
many out, and there was not much to do after it was
over. We provided that concert venue for after the
market and helped make Thursdays a fun night out. Our
concerts are over by 9:30 or 10 p.m., and people can still
get home at a decent hour. We found our niche. We
also discovered we could get high-caliber artists (some
of whom were Grammy winners and National Heritage
Fellows) for an affordable price because the scale was
lower for folk artists than for pop, jazz, or classical artists. And folk artists were happy to have a place in our
region supporting them.

In our galleries and classes, we noticed that we were
one of only a handful of places in southern California
that honored fine craft skills and taught fine craft programs. Since we are a 1924 Arts and Crafts-era building,

we decided to own this distinction and take the position that we are part of a movement trying to restore
and reinterpret the Arts and Crafts movement. Ethnic
dance and music were a big part of this movement
into the 1920s and led to the establishment of modern
dance in the 1940s. Now we have an identity.

It was these ethnic folk music and dance concerts
through evaluation that led to a great new identity for
the Muck. When I started in 2007, the Muck hosted a
jazz series of four concerts and a Shakespeare play for
ten performances. The total audience for all fourteen
shows was just over five hundred people. Last year we
hosted sixty-five concerts, most of which sold out for a
total of over eleven thousand attendees. This amazing
growth came only through planning and evaluation of
programs, while developing programs that forged a new
identity for us.

Accentuate the Positive

The Johnny Mercer song, "Accentuate the Positive" is
a great guide for developing and evaluating programs.
Unless the program is dreadfully wrong, you usually are
tweaking them more than scrapping them. After you
evaluate the program:

> You've got to accentuate the positive,
> Eliminate the negative,
> Latch on to the affirmative,
> And don't mess with Mister In-Between.

You've got to spread joy up to the maximum,
Bring gloom down to the minimum,
Have faith or pandemonium's
Liable to walk upon the scene

Review
Successful programs:

- Serve the mission *substantially*
- Require great leadership
- Are successful because they are well used
- Have a vision, plan, and goals addressed annually
- Eventually generate their own support
- Are well documented and evaluated

If you are not on this path, you must re-evaluate your programs.

Reporting and Evaluating Progress:
Successes and Challenges

True Genius resides in the capacity for evaluation of
uncertain, hazardous and conflicting information.
—Winston Churchill

I t will be your reports and evaluations of your programs that keep stakeholders and the community
in touch with the mission and vision of the organization. We must report both the successes and the challenges in a way that drives more interest and growth
in the mission. Evaluation is the difference between
a stagnant organization and a vibrant one because
evaluation leads to positive change. If you drive a car
that makes a weird noise and you never look at it to
see what is going on, you run the risk of having a car
break down or blow up on you. You won't know what
it is until you evaluate it. I'm not saying your organization is making a weird noise. But don't be one of
those people who fix it by turning the radio up louder.
That is exactly what you do when you don't evaluate

your programs. Everything we use in life would be substandard if it were never tested and improved. Yet so many non-profits go years without every checking under the hood to see if they are doing the best to serve the mission.

There are four basic tools we use for evaluation:

- Client surveys
- Staff and volunteer surveys
- Statistics
- Documentation

Each is important, and each serves a different purpose in evaluating your organization, programs, and goals.

Client Surveys

If you want to know how your program is going, you must ask the people using it. However, if the person administering the program asks, are the clients going to be honest? They like the program and the person administering it. They don't want to hurt his or her feelings. Therefore, if you want accurate feedback, it's important to find a way to ask for honest answers without their fearing you will be upset with them. This can be done a variety of ways.

Have an outside neutral party do the evaluation orally or in writing. If they promise that the information will be kept confidential, people will tell the truth.

Create an anonymous written survey. In this way people don't have to feel worried that what they say may come back to haunt them. There are many good ways to do this online (again, we use www.surveymonkey.com) or in person with college interns distributing the survey as a project for the school.

Survey the clients incognito. If the clients don't know who you are as CEO because you haven't been by the program in a while and you have a transitional group, it's possible you can do the survey because they do not yet know you. I get to play *Undercover Boss*. I will casually and quietly enter an event in the back and act like a new client or volunteer. I'll say, "Is this a good program? What do you like about it?" By the time someone points out that I am the director, I have received the critique of the program. The client will feel bad and start backtracking. "I didn't mean to act as if it were a bad program, I just thought that could be better. I'm sorry." I put them at ease and say, "It's OK. I am looking for real feedback. That's why I didn't tell you who I was. Do you think programs get better if they don't get honest feedback? Because you were so honest with me, I want to give you some tickets to our concert next week." The next thing you know, everyone in the room is giving honest feedback because they see I rewarded the first person for giving it.

Staff and Volunteer Evaluations

Staff and volunteers presumably give you honest feed-

back all the time in your inner circle meetings and when
asked. By this time, you have created a culture where
people feel they can be honest with you even if they
disagree. However, you can check that by doing an occa-
sional anonymous survey online or through the board.
Your board should evaluate you annually as you do your
staff and getting feedback from your staff about you
and the programs. Many people get nervous when staff
members talk directly to board without going through
the CEO. However, if your culture is set up as we have
discussed here, you will have nothing to worry about.

Statistics

One of the most difficult, important, and overlooked
parts of programming is keeping accurate and up-to-
date statistics on your programs and organization. It's
often just not done or is "guesstimated." I must admit
"guesstimating" from time to time when my staff members have fallen short on keeping accurate statistics.
How can you grow or even know what your programs
do without accurate numbers?

Do you keep records of how many attend your programs and any key demographic information on them?
For example, if you have a grant to increase Latino
participation at your programs, do you know how many
Latinos are participating? Do you know how many come
from within your service area? Do you know the staff/
client ratio?

If you know these things you can figure out how

many dollars you spend on each client and on each hour of service. You will know how much is directly invested in programs and how much is in administrating the program. You can track whether your clients are growing or shrinking in population, and whether the demographics are shifting significantly. All of these things will affect how you fundraise, program, and develop your goals.

Good statistics can dramatically grow a program, and bad ones can reveal opportunities to dramatically improve a program. Both are opportunities for new funds and for improving your mission. Don't fall in the trap of thinking a negative number is bad and makes you look bad. A number is just a number. It's how you interpret its meaning, and what your response is to it, that will determine the outcome.

Three years ago we realized that our classes were shrinking at the Muck quite significantly. Internally, we had a struggle going on. I had resisted making changes to the education component of our program because of staffing issues I inherited and a more urgent need to fix another program. After two years the other issues were fixed and the staffing problems were being resolved, but our education programs had suffered.

Now I was free to work as I wanted, but the pressure was on with my board to produce and show I had made the right decisions in dealing with the staffing issues and schedule. In our annual report that year, everything was way up and doing well except education. I didn't hide it. I put the stats in the annual report and explained that we were in the process of revamping this program. Our numbers had gone from 1700 students to under 1000. My decision to make this public caused more problems internally with some who felt that we should hide it or that the figures must somehow be wrong.

One of our major investors called to say that she was very proud of our report and my decision to put the negative number in. She was impressed that we weren't trying to hide it. Over the next three years, we were able to implement a new outreach program that grew out of the changes in our educational programs. We went from receiving no grants to receiving approximately $200,000 a year in grant funding for education and outreach. We went from one site at the Muck to serving eight sites all over the region. By 2014, we will serve twelve sites. In three years our education programs have gone from just under one thousand to over eight thousand students each year, an 800 percent increase. The moral to this story: if you do what is right even when things look bad, everything will come out right in the end.

Statistical Analysis

Having accurate statistics isn't enough. The real science, as Churchill said, is interpreting them. You see a trend, but what does the trend mean? The only way you can know this is by combining what you learn from surveys with what you learn from statistics. If Latino participation is down, is that because of a problem in your program, a positive change in your program that has diversified the demographics more, or a change in community demographics? You can't know without the survey information. Maybe Latino participation is down because the neighborhood is becoming more African American and Latinos are moving out. Maybe it's because you were not serving the African American community enough before, and now that you are serving them more, some of those slots that were Latino have changed. Maybe your staff members are all English speakers and the Chicano population that used to live there has given way to a more immigrant Latino population that doesn't speak English. So they have stopped participating. Each of these outcomes would have a different new goal for the program in terms of participation.

How would the program's investors feel to know not just the demographic shift, but your analysis of it and the new goal you've set because of it? If they just had the statistics, they might discontinue funding of the program. The analysis breathes life into the statistics. They may increase their funding knowing that you are on top of the trends.

This might be a report filed in South Florida a year after the earthquake in Haiti: "In evaluating our after-school soccer program for elementary schools, we found that Latino participation is down 20 percent while West Indian immigrant families are up 10 percent. We did not find this same shift to be true in high schools. After conducting a survey of participants, we found that many families in the Latino community are moving to the new housing project built in the Westside, while six new Haitian families have moved in through a church sponsorship. Some of our Spanish-speaking volunteers and staff are also considering a move to the Westside. We have decided to find and groom a new staff member who is familiar with the West Indian Community from our volunteer ranks. John Smith is from Haiti and has volunteered with us for two years. He is great with the younger kids. We ask that our investors consider increasing next year's grant to pay for the new stipend of $5,000 a year. We will keep a watch on this new demographic trend and see how it affects the program."

Documentation

Documenting your programs in pictures and video isn't just a nice thing to do for old times' sake. Documentation is the third rail of evaluation. If it's not there, nothing will power your program. Investors, board, and staff live to see the fruits of their labor. These pictures tell a tale of your program.

Client letters are also very important, whether they are kids writing in crayon or adults testifying on paper about how your program changed their lives. Sometimes the letters clients write are wonderfully insightful documents telling you that you were accomplishing something you didn't even know you were doing. I have received letters from clients thanking me for mentoring them, and I didn't even think they had noticed I existed. (Teenagers have a way of acting as if they are not listening when they are hanging on every word.)

When taking pictures or videos, make sure you have written releases and permission to use those pictures, especially if they are minors. You don't want to publish a picture of a kid who is in hiding in a battered women's shelter from an abusive dad or a picture of a women who is being stalked by a psychopath. If getting permission is a problem because you work with people who can't or shouldn't give their permission, you can always photograph them from the back participating in the program.

Making Your Reports

Reports, like brochures, say a great deal about you and your organization. The two biggest projects our marketing director works on each year are our annual brochure and our annual report. We treat them equally in terms of weight. Both are responsible for the community's view of us as an organization. The brochure goes out to everyone as a calling card of who we are and what we do. Every year from September to December, the brochure is the top priority for our marketing department (a director and interns). From June through September, the focus shifts to the annual report, which goes to all our investors, members, stakeholders, and also our potential investors. If the brochure is our stage, the annual report is a peek behind the curtain for those VIPs who get to see how the show runs.

Therefore, our annual report must be as beautiful as the brochure, with knock-your-socks-off statistics, documentation, and analysis. The good things must be accented. The challenges must show how we will overcome them. This document has attitude! It says we are doing amazing things and overcoming great obstacles to serve this community—and we love doing it!

Usually, the report has a cover photo that sets the tone of the report. For example, one year we wanted to highlight the awards we had won, so we chose a cover photo of our most prestigious award with our iconic building behind it. Another year we wanted to highlight our great strides in education, so we chose a picture of a teacher doing something great with his students (with our iconic building behind him). Compose this image wisely because it's the opening of the theme you are trying to convey. If you are saying in your report that you are proud of your diversity and your cover is a picture of all white people doing a program, you are sending a mixed message. (I actually saw this happen on a report of a peer organization once).

Inside may or may not be a table of contents, depending on the size of the report. There will usually be a letter from the director. This is your chance to highlight things you want the reader to focus on and give an overview of the year in a nutshell. The mission statement is featured prominently, as is the history, a list of staff and board with short biographies of key staff members and board executives.

After your letter, you might consider some nice charts showing growth, statistics showing improvement, bullet points showing successes and challenges, and photos documenting your program successes. You might have a list of programs from the year and a list of planned programs for next year with a blurb about next year's goals and projections. A budget page will show your organization's budget comparing it to last year and a projection for next year. There may be a page of notes explaining great rises or falls in budget, other big changes or anticipated changes, and new sources of income. This report isn't the place to be shy. It's your annual chance to brag.

Most organizational bylaws call for an annual meeting with members or stakeholders. It's best to make this report coincide with your annual meeting so you can pass out the report and present a report of your great successes and optimistic plans for the future. Bring out your star clients and showcase their successes. This is a great opportunity to connect stakeholders to the mission and inspire them. Accent your presentation with appropriate jokes, inspirational quotes, graphs showing your meteoric rise, and funny pictures as metaphors for new goals. Make it fun and exciting, but most of all, give stakeholders credit for the successes and show them how, thanks to their support, you will overcome the challenges. This is a celebration of your team.

When I started at the Muck, patrons received a mailing once each year, and that was it. Our season was only three months, with fewer than twenty events. Now our stakeholders get the big annual meeting and report in September, where we can show off our great successes and our eighty annual events. Our concert season runs through November, with a fall fundraiser included. Then in December they receive their annual brochure in the mail or at our holiday event showcasing the exciting new season. In January we close for renovations. The first week of February, we host a big ribbon cutting for the things we've renovated and showcase again our new season. From January through April, I am touring around town speaking at social service clubs and chamber events about our exciting new programs. In May, we hold a big fundraiser and a series of free festivals through the summer. In summer we do a second mailing showcasing our summer series and summer kids' camps. In September it starts all over again.

Now we are serving our mission year-round, and we remind our stakeholders constantly of our programs before, during, and after they occur. The fact we are doing much more is compounded by the fact we are reporting it much more, so it actually seems as if we are doing three times the work. Stakeholders constantly ask me, "How do you do all these things you do?" To which I reply, "With your help!"

Review

There are four tools for evaluation:

1. Client surveys
2. Staff and volunteer surveys
3. Statistics
4. Documentation

The annual brochure, website, and annual report are the most important tools for marketing. Make sure they include evaluation findings that support your mission.

Annual meetings are also great opportunities to connect the mission with stakeholders.

Information from evaluation is also used in press releases, grant reports and applications, and board reports.

At this point you have passed your hundred days. You spent your first fifty days setting up the leadership, mission, and vision for the organization and getting everyone on board. You spent your last fifty days networking in the community; fixing programs, tweaking staff, board and volunteers to make a better organization; and raising awareness, which raises funds. You are documenting and evaluating your work. Now it's time to think about succession. Even though your organization will never want you to leave after you've turned it around so dramatically, your obligation is to be ready for anything. No one lives forever or is director forever. You must ensure the organization will continue to prosper after you leave.

Succession Planning:
Making Your Success Outlive You

Why succession planning failed in the kingdom of Wakka-Wakka.

There are two lasting bequests we can hope to give our children. One of these is roots and the other, wings.
—Hodding Carter II (Pulitzer Prize-winning journalist, civil rights leader, and World War II veteran.)

Your hundred days have come and gone. Once you've been successful at growing your non-profit, it's important to ensure that when you leave, your work will not be in vain because your successor dismantled your programs and ideas.

You have the same responsibility to your non-profit that parents have to their children: to leave them with an inheritance that allows them to prosper after you are gone. If you can leave your non-profit with leaders you have a sense of history and a faith in their wings, they will fly far beyond what you have established Established companies, religions, monarchies, and governments all owe their longevity to succession planning. It's the only way to keep your successes going after you are gone.

Training Leaders

The first responsibility in succession planning is training good leaders among your board, your volunteers, your staff, and your clients. They call it "succession" because you are grooming leaders for "success." Most successful organizations stay that way when the next leaders are brought up within the organizations. If you noticed, through the book we have talked about recruiting key leaders for programs, committees, and our inner circle. These are your hopefuls for taking over for you and the board one day. You must make sure they learn what you have learned about LMV.

Leaving Information

You should have a policy that every staff member has a one-page document describing how to access that person's information in the event of an emergency. It should include their passwords, where they keep important files, contacts, current information on projects, and so on. The information should be written down and kept in a locked location, in a sealed envelope for emergency use only. This way staff members don't have to feel that you are going through their stuff. You must do this for your information as well and give it to your board president. It's kind of a "last will and testament" for work. Should you be hit by a bus or win the lottery and not come back, people could go on without having to decipher all your information and start from scratch.

I was in a situation in which my second in command

was going through a tough personal situation at home and quit with no notice. It took us weeks to get access to her files and days to figure out what she was doing and how to access it. Meanwhile clients and staff were waiting for things. If we had had this paper in place, the transition could have been smoother.

Having a Second in Command

Most small and mid-sized non-profits are not large enough to afford a dedicated director of operations. In most places the CEO is also the COO. We usually wear two or three more hats as well. But that doesn't mean you can't have a second in command. This would be a person who is capable of filling in for you when necessary. It would be someone you are grooming for your job. This person can fill in for you when you are sick or on vacation and handle the day-to-day things that come up.

Having a second almost permits you the opportunity to pick your own successor—someone you have groomed in a way that works for the organization. Should you get another position and must leave, the board will feel good knowing you have set them up for the transition. You can tell them you have prepared for a smooth transition. Your second can be an acting CEO for six months to a year while they do a search. You can offer to sit on the board or advisory board to help smooth the transition because you care about the mission. If your protégé is as good as you hope, he or

she should have a great shot at keeping the job in the
long run.

Grooming a Successor

Remember that the big difference between an operations director or second in command and you is that
the second is responsible for the day-to-day events. You
are the one creating the vision for the future, setting
the tone, leading the group, and networking in the
community. Therefore, it's important when grooming a
staff member to become a successor that you help that
person focus on his or her weaknesses. A second must
be good at public speaking, schmoozing, and networking. Does your person have the capacity for that kind
of social interaction? He or she will need the ability
to think ahead, gather consensus, and plan the vision
for the organization's future. Can your successor think
strategically and see the opportunities and challenges
down the road?

Chances are you are not going to find your perfect
successor. If someone had your exact same qualities,
there would have been no reason to hire that person.
You would just have a duplicate of yourself. Also, someone with your personality would most likely clash with
you. It takes a strong personality or someone who has a
quiet strength to lead. It's possible you don't see a staff
member who is equipped to lead. A good second in
command doesn't always make a good commander. But
among your staff, you certainly have a team of people

who can replace you. Maybe one staff member is great at leading in the office but horrible at networking in public, afraid of public speaking. Another is great with public speaking and networking but horrible at administration. The two together might be a good solution as "co-acting directors" until a director is hired.

Staying Involved through the Transition

By offering to sit on the board for a year during the transition, you ensure that the organization will transition in a way that will ensure your legacy isn't damaged. You can be involved in picking the interim director from your staff and picking the director to replace you. This also helps the organization you helped build. No one on the board knows what the organization needs to continue its growth the way you know.

Don't feel you must pick a leader from your staff if there isn't one who is qualified for the permanent job. Also, don't feel that you must pick a leader who is just like you. Just help them pick a leader with a great attitude and a commitment to LMV: someone with leadership qualities, who cares about the mission, and who is a visionary and strategic thinker. Use your networks to help recruit candidates you admired from strategic partners. Make sure that the interview process for a replacement involves samples of their writing and their ability to give public presentations. Someone who doesn't interview well may not do well in public speaking either.

Having an Incoming Board President

It's important that you work with your board to ensure they have an incoming president picked even while the current president is still serving. In some cases the position might be called a vice president. If something happens to your president with whom you have worked so hard forging a great relationship, anything can happen. If you have helped put in place a successor, you know what to expect and hopefully have a great relationship with that person.

One day your president decides to move out of state because his or her daughter is having a baby and has moved across country. The president is retired and wants to spend time with the grandchildren. This sends the board into a tizzy. No one who is qualified wants to be president, and the person screaming to do it is the one person you are most afraid of having that much power. It's the one board member who thinks his or her every idea is golden and everyone else's ideas are dumb. This person is often heard saying, "If I were president, we would do things differently. We don't need to spend money on all these fancy brochures, networking lunches, and a flashy website. My nephew should run this place. He'd straighten things up." Now, not only are you in trouble, but the whole organization you spent years setting up is in jeopardy. This could all have been avoided by having a president-elect ready to go.

Planning Staff Succession

Your staff members need succession plans too. It may

not be a written document. However, as a visionary thinker, you should know in your head what you would do in the event each of your staff members were to resign. The question isn't simply "How would I conduct interviews for a replacement and who would do the job in the interim?" That is easy enough to determine with these questions.

Should I replace this person at all?

In some cases the employee might be doing a job a contractor could fill. It may be the case that a full-time job is no longer warranted and could be replaced by a part-time position. In other cases the employee might be in a position you inherited for a program that you are ending. It might not need filling at all. In other cases it could be filled by a volunteer. Because money in non-profits is always tight, make sure you need to fill the position before you move on.

Has the position changed?

This position may have become more or less important over the years. It could be folded in with another position or become bumped up to a higher-level position. Maybe you had two program managers and need only one now. Or maybe your development associate needs to be bumped up to a development director position.

Could this be an opportunity for a reorganization of staff?

Sometimes when a high-level manager leaves, there is

an opportunity to reorganize staff more efficiently. For example, when I started at the Muck, we had a staff of three managers—the executive director (me), an operations manager, and a curator. When the operations manager left, her salary was large enough for us to hire two managers who were at the start of their careers and train them. So we promoted a part-time staff member to be a full-time office manager and hired a new marketing director, which we sorely needed. This one move did more to improve our growth than any other hiring decisions we made. The office manager blossomed into a great administrative director. In time we recruited an education director from grants and contracts for new classes. Now we have seven managers, with the addition of a lead artist and an events manager.

Should I Hire Someone Who Is Experienced Or a Trainee?

You might have a high-salaried employee who leaves. Given the position, is it more prudent to hire another experienced person with a high salary or consider training someone at a much lower salary and using the difference to fill other staffing needs?

Remember that training staff usually makes them better because they are trained in your own image and likeness. But training takes time and money, and there is no guarantee that people won't leave you once you've trained them. If the need is urgent or very crucial to the mission, it might be more prudent to pay for a more experienced person who can hit the ground running.

So as you watch your staff work, from time to time ask yourself, what would I do if this person left me tomorrow? What opportunities would that open up for me, and what challenges would I face?

Review

- The first responsibility in succession planning is training good leaders to succeed you.
- Have your staff create a "last will and testament" for work that documents their responsibilities.
- Have a well-trained second in command.
- Train them to think strategically and network.
- Stay involved through the transition by offering to remain on the board for a year after you resign.
- Make sure your board has a president-elect in place.
- Make mental notes of staff succession strategies for all key roles.
- Should staff resign, ask yourself:
  — Should I replace this person at all?
  — Has the position changed?
  — Could this be an opportunity for a reorganization of staff?
  - Should I hire someone who is experienced or a trainee?

T hanks for reading my book. I hope this book has
been helpful to you. I am happy to work with
anyone reading this book who needs more mentoring as
time permits. You can reach me at zoot@themuck.org.
To find out more about The Muck or its programs, visit
themuck.org.

The LMV Toolbox

Twenty tools for a successful organization:

1. **This Book.**
2. **Staff handbook with policy memos.** A clear employee handbook with rules, training, benefits, and staff members' signatures showing that they have read it. See Chapter 2 on staff.
3. **Staff evaluations.** A method to evaluate staff periodically. This might include a regimen for training, raises, and team building. See Chapter 2 on staff.
4. **Needs assessment.** An academic-style study of the community needs for which your mission is designed and how you are addressing them with facts, statistics, and anecdotes. See Chapter 3 on mission.
5. **Mission statement.** A clear, concise, and measurable statement of your mission as agreed upon by consensus. See Chapter 3 on mission.
6. **Board bylaws.** Must be reviewed and discussed. These are your friend, as they can help you in board development and keeping the board accountable.

See Chapter 4 on board.

7. **Strategic plan with:**
   a. **Retreat.** An important tool in consensus build-
      ing with stakeholders. See Chapter 5 on vision.
   b. **Backward timeline.** A way to calculate a three-
      year plan or any plan by starting with the end
      goal and working backward in time until the
      present. See Chapter 5 on vision.
   c. **SWOT analysis.** An assessment of your organiza-
      tion's strengths, weaknesses, opportunities, and
      threats. See Chapter 5 on vision.
   d. **Three-year goals and objectives.** See Chapter 5
      on vision.
   e. **Strategic plan budget.** A projected budget that
      matches your three-year goals and the interven-
      ing years' goals. See Chapter 5 on vision.

8. **Resource map.** A complete database of local,
   potential strategic partners such as all local non-
   profits, granting agencies, government agencies, and
   businesses. See Chapter 6 on Networks.

9. **Investor packet.** A packet for potential investors to
   reinforce your networking message to investors and
   get them interested in finding out more. It's both
   a PDF and physical brochure, folder, or binder. See
   Chapter 7 on fundraising.

10. **Grant application outline** (five Ws and four Hs). A
    simple outline for grant proposal writing. Great for
    training staff. See Chapter 7 on fundraising.

11. **Logo.** A clear, simple, and concise one. See Chapter
    8 on marketing.

12. **Website.** One of your most important tools. This is how many people will find you. It needs to be amazing, simple, and beautiful. See Chapter 8 on marketing.

13. **Annual brochure.** A great brochure is how many people will find you. It needs to be amazing, simple, and beautiful, like your website. See Chapter 8 on marketing.

14. **E-blasts and social media.** You must stay in regular communication with your stakeholders, and in the twenty-first century, that means e-blasts and status updates on social media. See Chapter 8 on marketing.

15. **Program plans.** Outline a program's goals and objectives and update them regularly based on evaluations. See Chapter 9 on programs.

16. **Surveys.** Evaluation is important to grow successful programs, and surveys are an important tool for that. See Chapter 10 on evaluation and reports.

17. **Photo and video documentation.** A picture is worth a thousand words. Short videos are excellent content for websites, YouTube channels, and social media. See Chapter 10 on evaluation and reports.

18. **Brochure.** This is your organization's calling card and describes who you are and what you do. It is the community's view of you as an organization. See Chapter 10 on evaluation and reports.

19. **Annual report.** Potential investors, grantors, stakeholders, and community members will see this. A great annual report is the hallmark of a suc-

cessful organization. See Chapter 10 on evaluation and reports.

20. **Succession plan.** Don't be caught in shock when a staff member or board member leaves, and plan for your legacy at the organization. See the Epilogue on succession planning.

100-Day Timeline

10 Days In: Undertake Fact Finding

- Become an expert on the organization.
- Interview stakeholders.
- Assess culture.

20 Days In: Set Up Your Inner Circle

- Meet with key stakeholders to announce findings.
- Set up a strategic planning retreat.
- Conduct a needs assessment.
- Start networking in the community.

30 Days In: Set Up Community Ties

- Join the most obvious networks for strategic partners and mentors.
- Ensure staff training is underway with team building

and incentive programs.

- Strengthen board relationships with you training them as they mentor you.

40 Days In: Prepare for Change

- Plan the retreat.
- Finish the strategic plan.
- Conduct a resource map and expand your networks.
- Handle staff changes, new hires, and other staffing decisions.
- Plan the website and marketing to reflect new changes in the strategic plan.
- Ensure that a new brochure is in the works.
- Find seed investors to fund the changes.

50 Days In: Carry Out the Strategic Plan Approved by the Board

- Publish and network the plan.
- Set up tours of your organization with potential investors from your networks.
- Speak at community networks about the new exciting plan.
- Implement new programs (or needed changes to programs and staffing).
- Set timelines with the staff for marketing, fundraising, grants, program changes, and so on.

70 Days In: Evaluate

- Start evaluation of changes—surveys and stats.
- Make changes and tweaks accordingly.
- Use stats for more investment from stakeholders and networks.

80 Days In: Prepare for Growth

- Expand on or change programs from evaluation.
- Prepare grants and reports on changes.
- Work with staff to complete a marketing strategy.
- Work with the board to complete a fundraising strategy.
- Work with networks to increase interest in the mission and new goals.
- Evaluate stakeholders' handling of the changes.

90 Days In: Manage Growth

- Evaluate staff performance.
- Evaluate volunteer and board needs.
- Evaluate network needs.
- Delegate things that can be delegated to staff.
- Train your delegates.

100 Days In: Continue with Vision and Supervision

- Ensure that many day-to-day tasks have been delegated.
- Prioritize networks, and delegate the lower-priority networks to staff and the board.
- Spend time on important networks, one-on-one meetings with investors and board, vision planning, evaluation of plans and goals, supervision of staff deadlines, handling crises, and setting future goals.

Early in your hundred days, you were doing all the work and setting up your staff members and other stakeholders to be delegates. Later in your hundred days, you had a well-trained group of delegates doing the work. You are very involved supervising them, checking to be sure they meet their deadlines. You're networking and continuing to forge partnerships and find investors that will grow the organization. You manage with vision, always thinking about future— repercussions of today's actions, partnerships, headlines, and so on.

After 100 Days

Before, 60 to 75 percent of your time was training and managing staff and programs. Now the staff are trained, and programs are running more successfully. Your calendar has become more manageable. You're working a forty- to fifty-hour week, spending 60 percent of your time in the community networking and meeting board and investors, and 40 percent of your time supervising staff and programs. If you have a great inner circle, you might even be spending a little less time supervising.

Evaluations are constant. Programs are growing and changing. The budget is also growing as the mission grows. Your job becomes more focused on meeting and clearing way for the growth. Cycles repeat with new strategic plans, program plans, reports, brochures, web tweaks, and networking. Soon you are doing things you never dreamed you could do. The only limits are your imagination.

About the Author

Zoot's life is defined by one event. At 10 days old, Zoot was burned over 80% of his body in a house fire. He spent the next five years living in a hospital and had over a hundred surgeries before graduating high school. Despite losing all the muscles in his right leg below the knee, he made a 12-year career as a professional break dancer, mime, actor and storyteller. He received a bachelor's degree in dance from St. Mary's College. He also holds professional designations in arts education, fundraising, management and conflict resolution. He has appeared in commercials, films and television shows with Michael Jackson, Prince, Arsenio Hall, James Cameron, and many others; and toured his one-man shows internationally at venues such as the Kennedy Center, The National Theater, Wolf Trap, The Music Center, Japan's Canal City and Spoleto International Theater Festival. His passion for teaching brought him to schools, juvenile halls, prisons, malls and hospitals under 16 grants and numerous commissions. His three years of arts residencies

with gang members in prisons and schools culminated
in co-creating the 1992 California Arts Council-Los
Angeles Riot Recovery Program in Watts and the 1994
Los Angeles Earthquake Recovery Program with the Los
Angeles Cultural Affairs Department.

He transferred from artist to administrator when
he managed a prison arts program creating the first
inmate music CDs produced in prison, the first youth
deterrent program in the form of a play, and hand made
books in museum collections at the Getty, Hammer and
Library of Congress. In 2000, he managed all cultural
programs in the Harbor area and opened four new
art centers for the City of Los Angeles Cultural Affairs
Department. A Certified Fund Raising Executive (CFRE),
he has raised more than $10 million for various non-
profits. In 2007, he became the executive director of
the Muckenthaler Cultural Center in Fullerton, Calif.
He doubled the budget and tripled the organization's
programs in just three years during the worst depression
since the 1930s. He received a Community Leadership
Fellowship award from the state of California and a City
of Pasadena Fellowship and commendations for his
community work in Los Angeles, Long Beach, Ventura,
Oxnard, and Fullerton. He has authored plays, poems,
and coauthored the book "The Muckenthaler Cultural
Center" (from the "Images of America" series, published
by Arcadia Publishing).